Study Guide

Richard Moriarty

CULINARY
FUNDAMENTALS

THE AMERICAN CULINARY FEDERATION

PEARSON

Prentice
Hall

Upper Saddle River, New Jersey 07458

Pearson Prentice Hall™ is a trademark of Pearson Education, Inc.
Pearson® is a registered trademark of Pearson plc
Prentice Hall® is a registered trademark of Pearson Education, Inc.

Pearson Education LTD.
Pearson Education Singapore, Pte. Ltd.
Pearson Education Canada, Ltd.
Pearson Education–Japan
Pearson Education Australia PTY, Limited
Pearson Education North Asia Ltd.
Pearson Educación de Mexico, S.A. de C.V.
Pearson Education Malaysia, Pte. Ltd.

10 9 8
ISBN 0-13-118013-4

For all the culinary students who dream of becoming chefs, and for the teachers who help them achieve their dreams. And for my three sons, Shawn, Jack and Matt, who keep me young.

—Richard Moriarty

Contents

UNIT 1
PROFESSIONALISM

A. Terminology: Fill in the blank space with the correct definition.

1. chef _____

2. culinarian _____

3. brigade system _____

4. certification _____

5. degree _____

6. formal education _____

7. networking _____

8. professionalism _____

9. Grande Cuisine _____

10. Cuisine Classique _____

11. Nouvelle Cuisine _____

12. global cooking _____

B. Fill in the Blank: Fill in the blank with the word that best completes the sentence.

1. A _____ makes a living from the practice of a craft.

2. Acquiring the skills and knowledge necessary to succeed in culinary arts takes how long? _____

3. The best culinary schools offer plenty of _____.

4. A means of measuring and quantifying the achievements of a chef is through _____.

5. _____ was brought to court for infringing on a guild's monopoly by offering his customers a dish of sheep's feet in white sauce.

6. _____ wrote *Le Guide Culinaire.*

7. Chef Fernand Point is associated with _____ Cuisine.

8. Escoffier's brigade system was instituted to _____ and _____ work in hotel kitchens.

9. The second in command in the kitchen is the _____.

10. The pantry chef is also known as the _____.

C. Short Answer: Provide a short response that correctly answers each question below.

1. List 3 examples of what a professional culinarian must learn.

   a. _____

   b. _____

   c. _____

2. List 3 aspects of good service that professional culinarians should be committed to providing their customers.

   a. _____

   b. _____

   c. _____

3. List 3 criteria a culinarian must meet in order to receive certification.

    a. _____

    b. _____

    c. _____

4. List 4 chefs who were influenced by Fernand Point and are credited with inventing nouvelle cuisine during the early 1970s.

    a. _____

    b. _____

    c. _____

    d. _____

D. Culinary Trends: Match each of the chefs in List A with the culinary accomplishment or trend that person is associated with.

List A	*List B*
___ 1. Apicus	a. Cuisine Classique, *Le Guide Culinaire*
___ 2. M. Boulanger	b. Grande Cuisine, cooking for nobility
___ 3. Marie-Antoine Careme	c. Nouvelle Cuisine, La Pyramide
___ 4. Cesar Ritz	d. wrote one of first cookbooks for chefs
___ 5. Georges-Auguste Escoffier	e. served sheep's feet in white sauce
___ 6. Fernand Point	f. Savoy Hotel, Haute cuisine

E. Matching: Match each of the terms in List A with the appropriate job description in List B.

List A	*List B*
___ 1. chef de cuisine	a. responsible for all fried foods
___ 2. sous chef	b. responsible for all sautéed items
___ 3. sauté chef (saucier)	c. works as needed throughout the kitchen

___ 4. fish chef (poissonier)   d. is responsible for all grilled foods

___ 5. roast chef (rôtisseur)   e. works under a chef de partie

___ 6. grill chef (grillardin)   f. prepares the meal served to staff

___ 7. fry chef (friturier)   g. last to see the plate before it leaves the kitchen

___ 8. vegetable chef (entremetier)   h. second in command

___ 9. roundsman (tournant)   i. responsible for all kitchen operations

___10. expediter (aboyeur)   j. is responsible for all roasted foods

___11. communard   k. is responsible for hot appetizers

___12. commis   l. is responsible for fish items and their sauces

F. Multiple Choice: For each question, choose the one correct answer.

1. This chef frequently supervises a separate kitchen area or a separate shop in larger operations.
    a. sous chef
    b. pastry chef
    c. executive chef
    d. cold-foods chef

2. This culinarian oversees all food and beverage outlets in hotels and other large establishments.
    a. roundsman
    b. chef de cuisine
    c. food and beverage manager
    d. station chef

3. Typically, an executive chef is responsible for:
    a. all kitchen operations
    b. scheduling
    c. development of menu items
    d. all of the above

4. Which of the following requirements is not necessary to maintain a chef's certification?
   a. periodically refresh their knowledge in specific competencies and skills
   b. provide documentation of professional development
   c. participate in approved culinary salons
   d. secure employment in at least two restaurants that practice different cuisine styles

G. True or False: Circle either True or False to indicate the correct answer.

1. Everyone in a professional kitchen has a stake in keeping the customer happy.

   True   False

2. Hands-on practice and culinary theory is the same thing.

   True   False

3. Certification is not widely recognized as a statement of a chef's development.

   True   False

4. Tradition is an important part of the culinary profession.

   True   False

5. After the French Revolution professional chefs often went into business for themselves.

   True   False

6. Because of the high degree of organization involved in the Grande Cuisine style of cooking only a small number of cooks were needed.

   True   False

7. Nouvelle cuisine was inspired by traditions from Japan.

   True   False

8. Paul Bocuse was influenced mostly by his work with Georges-Auguste Escoffier.

   True   False

5

9. The culinary profession has not changed much since M. Boulanger was a
   Parisian tavern keeper in 1765.

   True   False

10. Full-service restaurants often operate on cycle menus.

    True   False

UNIT 1 ANSWER KEY

A. Terminology

All definitions can be found in the text.

B. Fill in the Blank

1. professional
2. a lifetime
3. hands-on application
4. certification
5. A Frenchman, M. Boulanger
6. Escoffier
7. Nouvelle
8. streamline, simplify
9. sous chef
10. cold-foods chef (garde-manger)

C. Short Answer

1. a. How to handle ingredients and equipment
   b. Benchmark techniques and recipes
   c. How to manage the operation of a kitchen

2. a. Quality items that are properly and safely prepared
   b. Foods that are appropriately flavored
   c. Foods that are attractively presented

3. a. Have a high level of work and educational experience
   b. Pass both a written and practical cooking or baking examination
   c. Complete coursework in food safety, nutrition, and supervisory management

4. a. Paul Bocuse
   b. Chapel Alain
   c. Francois Bise
   d. Pierre Troisgros

D. Culinary Trends

1. d
2. e
3. b
4. f

5. a
6. c

E. Matching

   1. i
   2. h
   3. b
   4. l
   5. j
   6. d
   7. a
   8. k
   9. c
   10. g
   11. f
   12. e

F. Multiple Choice

   1. b
   2. c
   3. d
   4. d

G. True or False

   1. True
   2. False
   3. False
   4. True
   5. True
   6. False
   7. True
   8. False
   9. False
   10. False

UNIT 2
NUTRITION

A. Terminology: Fill in the blank space with the correct definition.

1. amino acid _____

2. antioxidant _____

3. calorie _____

4. carbohydrates _____

5. cholesterol _____

6. complete proteins _____

7. complex carbohydrates _____

8. dietary cholesterol _____

9. empty calorie _____

10. fats _____

11. fiber _____

12. hydrogenation _____

13. minerals _____

14. nutrients _____

15. polyunsaturated fats _____

16. proteins _____

17. saturated fat _____

18. serum cholesterol _____

19. simple carbohydrates _____

20. trans fat _____

21. vitamins _____

B. Fill in the Blank: Fill in the blank with the word that best completes the sentence.

1. Nutrition is the study of _____.

2. In _____ the USDA introduced the first Food Guide Pyramid.

3. Fat calories should be limited to _____ percent of total daily calories.

4. A nutrient is considered essential if our bodies cannot

   _____.

5. Complex carbohydrates contain chains of sugars known as

   _____.

C. Short Answer: Provide a short response that correctly answers each question below.

1. List 4 ways water is critical to important chemical functions in the body.

   a. _____

   b. _____

   c. _____

   d. _____

2. List 3 ways to help retain water-soluble vitamins.

   a. _____

   b. _____

   c. _____

3. List 3 common foods that cause allergic reactions.

   a. _____

   b. _____

   c. _____

4. List 3 ways chefs can cook with fat wisely.

   a. _____

   b. _____

   c. _____

D. Matching: Match each of the terms in List A with the appropriate description in List B.

List A	*List B*
___1. USDA Food Guide Pyramid	a. a carbohydrate that humans cannot digest
___2. activity level	b. serum, or blood, cholesterol
___3. nutrient density	c. helps the body to absorb iron
___4. complex carbohydrates	d. presents a plan for a healthy diet
___5. fiber	e. plays a major role in determining how many calories a person should consume
___6. cholesterol measured in the blood	f. retinol
___7. cholesterol measured in food	g. sometimes referred to as "starches"
___8. Vitamin C	h. dietary cholesterol
___9. form of Vitamin A in plant food	i. the amount of nutrients a food source has in relation to the number of calories it contains
___10. form of Vitamin A in animal food	j. dark green, leafy vegetables

___11. a good source of Vitamin K   k. sodium and potassium

___12. minerals essential to regulating   l. beta-carotene
the body

E. Multiple Choice: For each question, choose the one correct answer.

1. Fiber is a form of:
   a. protein
   b. carbohydrate
   c. fat
   d. amino acid

2. Proteins should contribute what percent of total daily calories?
   a. 20 to 25
   b. 12 to 15
   c. 5 to 10
   d. 22 to 30

3. Excess fat in the diet can raise the risk of:
   a. coronary heart disease
   b. obesity
   c. certain cancers
   d. all of the above

4. All of the following are saturated fats *except*:
   a. butter
   b. lard
   c. coconut oil
   d. olive oil

5. When polyunsaturated fat is hydrogenated, it:
   a. becomes more saturated
   b. becomes less saturated
   c. becomes a liquid
   d. spoils faster

6. Dietary cholesterol is only found in:
   a. fish
   b. animal foods
   c. grains
   d. vegetables

UNIT 2 ANSWER KEY

A. Terminology

All definitions can be found in the text.

B. Fill in the Blank

  1. the foods we eat
  2. 1992
  3. 30
  4. manufacture it
  5. polysaccharides

C. Short Answer

  1. a. Dissolves water-soluble vitamins, minerals, and other compounds so
        they can travel through the bloodstream
     b. Removes impurities from the bloodstream and the body
     c. Cushions joints, organs, and sensitive tissues such as the spinal cord
     d. Maintains pressure on the optic nerves for proper vision

  2. a. Keep cooking times to a minimum
     b. Cook foods in as little water as possible or choose dry heat techniques like
        roasting
     c. Prepare foods as close to their time of service as possible

  3. a. Seafood
     b. Peanuts
     c. Wheat

  4. a. Know how much fat and what type of fat a food contains
     b. Replace saturated fats with either polyunsaturated fats or monounsaturated
        fats
     c. Look for interesting alternatives to sauces that contain butter or cream

D. Matching

  1. d
  2. e
  3. i
  4. g
  5. a
  6. b
  7. h

8. c
9. l
10. f
11. j
12. k

E. Multiple Choice

1. b
2. b
3. d
4. d
5. a
6. b

UNIT 3
SANITATION

A. Terminology: Fill in the blank space with the correct definition.

1. acidic food _____

2. bacteria _____

3. chemical contamination _____

4. contaminated food _____

5. cross contamination _____

6. danger zone_____

7. double-strength sanitizing solution _____

8. food borne illness _____

9. Hazard Analysis Critical Control Points (HACCP) _____

_____

10. pathogen _____

11. pH scale _____

12. physical contamination _____

13. potentially hazardous food _____

14. cleaning _____

15. sanitizing _____

16. toxins _____

17. two-stage cooling method _____

18. viruses _____

19. water activity (a_w) _____

B. Fill in the Blank: Fill in the blank with the word that best completes the sentence.

1. The number of food borne illnesses reported each year is nearly

   _____.

2. Bacteria can be carried by _____, _____,

   _____, _____, and

   _____.

3. _____ are cold-loving bacteria, destroyed by heat.

4. _____ are bacteria that thrive at moderate temperatures,

   destroyed by heat, slowed by cooling.

5. _____ are heat-loving bacteria, destroyed by cooling.

6. Molds and yeasts are types of _____.

7. Pathogens need _____ in order to grow and reproduce.

8. One of the most important elements in keeping foods safe is for food handlers

   to _____.

9. The transfer of pathogens from one food to another or from a work surface to

   a food is known as _____.

10. FIFO stands for _____.

C. Short Answer: Provide a short response that correctly answers each question below.

1. List 4 rules for safe foodhandling.

   a. _____

   b. _____

   c. _____

   d. _____

2. List 4 situations when food service employees should wash their hands.

   a. _____

   b. _____

   c. _____

   d. _____

3. List 6 ways to help prevent cross contamination.

   a. _____

   b. _____

   c. _____

   d. _____

   e. _____

   f. _____

D. Matching: Match each of the terms in List A with the appropriate description in List B.

List A	*List B*
___1. aerobic	a. developed for astronauts
___2. binary fission	b. destroyed by oxygen

17

___3. potentially hazardous foods   c. process when bacteria split in two

___4. anaerobic bacteria   d. have characteristics perfect for the development of food borne illness

___5. metal shavings in food   e. a chef's jacket

___6. HACCP   f. requires oxygen

___7. food borne infection   g. physical contamination

___8. facultative bacteria   h. caused by toxins

___9. double breasted cloth barrier   i. can adapt to either the presence of or the lack of oxygen

E. Multiple Choice: For each question, choose the one correct answer.

1. Each year, about _____ people die from a food borne illness.
   a. 4,000
   b. 7,000
   c. 9,000
   d. 12,000

2. Parasites depend upon _____ to survive.
   a. high acidity
   b. a living host
   c. low moisture content
   d. low temperatures

3. For sanitation purposes, hot-water ware-washing machines typically use water heated to:
   a. 180 degrees to 195 degrees F [82 degrees to 91 degrees C]
   b. 160 degrees to 175 degrees F [71 degrees to 79 degrees C]
   c. 195 degrees to 212 degrees F [91 degrees to 100 degrees C]
   d. 150 degrees to 165 degrees F [66 degrees to 74 degrees C]

4. After sanitizing, equipment and tableware should be:
   a. dried completely with clean paper towels
   b. dried completely with clean cloth towels
   c. allowed to air-dried completely
   d. stored immediately without drying

F. True or False: Circle either True or False to indicate the correct answer.

1. Pathogens are easy to detect because they affect the way foods look, smell, taste, and feel.

    True   False

2. Viruses in foods can survive freezing and cooking temperatures.

    True   False

3. The most favorable pH range for pathogens to grow is between 4.6 and 7.5.

    True   False

4. When thawing food under running water, maintain a water temperature of 85 degrees F. (29 degrees C) or below.

    True   False

5. When reheating foods they should reach a temperature of at least 165 degrees F (74 degrees C) for at least fifteen seconds within a four-hour time period.

    True   False

6. The heart of the HACCP system contains seven principles.

    True   False

7. A critical control point is the point in the process of food handling where you can prevent, eliminate, or reduce a hazard.

    True   False

8. Salt or cornmeal can be used to absorb spilled grease in the kitchen.

    Truc   False

9. To avoid becoming overheated, food service workers should wear short-sleeved jackets in the kitchen.

    True   False

10. When working in the kitchen, side towels should be used to wipe up spills on any work surface, as well as to protect your hands from hot surfaces.

    True   False

UNIT 3 ANSWER KEY

A. Terminology

   All definitions can be found in the text.

B. Fill in the Blank

   1. 76 million
   2. food, water, humans, animals, insects
   3. Phychrophiles
   4. Mesophiles
   5. Thermophiles
   6. fungus
   7. a food source
   8. wash their hands conscientiously and frequently
   9. cross contamination
   10. first in, first out

C. Short Answer

   1. a. Practice and require excellent personal hygiene.
      b. Identify potentially hazardous foods on the menu.
      c. Cook foods to safe internal temperatures, at a minimum, or higher.
      d. Reheat potentially hazardous foods to be held hot to an internal
         temperature of 165 degrees F within two hours.

   2. a. When arriving at work or returning to the kitchen
      b. After using the bathroom
      c. After smoking
      d. After handling garbage

   3. a. Keep raw and cooked foods in separate containers.
      b. Store cooked foods above raw foods.
      c. Clean and sanitize work surfaces and equipment when you move from one
         task to another.
      d. Keep foods at safe temperatures.
      e. Reheat foods quickly over direct heat, not in the steam table.
      f. Use the appropriate service utensil for each food.

D. Matching

   1. f
   2. c
   3. d

4. b
5. g
6. a
7. h
8. i
9. e

E. Multiple Choice

1. c
2. b
3. a
4. c

F. True or False

1. False
2. True
3. True
4. False
5. False
6. True
7. True
8. True
9. False
10. False

UNIT 4
FOOD SCIENCE BASICS

A. Terminology: Fill in the blank space with the correct definition.

1. convection _____

2. conduction _____

3. radiation _____

4. induction _____

5. microwave _____

6. infrared _____

7. caramelization _____

8. maillard reaction _____

9. gelatinization _____

10. denaturing proteins _____

11. coagulation _____

12. emulsion _____

13. rehydration _____

14. dehydration _____

15. smoke point _____

B. Fill in the Blank: Fill in the blank with the word that best completes the sentence.

1. At sea level, pure water freezes (becomes solid) at _____.

2. Generally, vegetable oils begin to smoke around _____,

   while animal fats begin to smoke around _____.

3. An important aspect of solutions is their pH, which is a measure of their

_____ or _____.

4. _____ pans are the best conductors of heat.

5. Thinner gauge pans conduct heat more _____ and respond

to temperature changes _____.

6. Thicker gauge pans hold heat and release it evenly and respond

_____ to temperature changes.

7. A vinaigrette is an example of an oil-in-water _____.

8. A temporary emulsion can be reformed by _____.

C. Short Answer: Provide a short response that correctly answers each question below.

1. How is the dehydration of foods accomplished?

_____

_____

2. How is the rehydration of foods accomplished?

_____

_____

3. What allows for the spongy texture in some cakes and makes whipped cream possible?

_____

_____

4. How can you prevent small clumps from forming in custard?

_____

_____

5. How does sugar act as a preservative?

_____

_____

6. List 3 cooking mediums.

a. _____

b. _____

c. _____

7. After food absorbs infrared radiation on the surface, what carries the heat to the center?

_____

_____

8. How does fat tenderize foods?

_____

_____

D. Matching: Match each of the terms in List A with the appropriate description in List B.

List A	List B
___1. temporary emulsion	a. slow method of heat transfer
___2. permanent emulsion	b. mayonnaise
___3. primary substance in fresh foods	c. stirring foods

___4. natural proteins   d. grilling over glowing coals

___5. complex carbohydrates   e. an alkali

___6. baking soda   f. vinaigrette

___7. lemon juice   g. water

___8. conduction   h. shaped like coils or springs

___9. mechanical convection   i. starches

___10. infrared radiation   j. an acid

E. True or False: Circle either True or False to indicate the correct answer.

1. Induction cooktops heat and cool rapidly.

       True   False

2. Induction cooktops have a coil that generates a magnetic current.

       True   False

3. Induction cooktops only work with pans that are non-ferrous; that is, they contain no iron.

       True   False

4. When food is cooked, only its flavor and texture change.

       True   False

5. Both caramelization and the Maillard reaction occur at temperatures below the boiling point of water.

       True   False

6. Butter is an example of a water-in-oil emulsion.

       True   False

7. High levels of sugar or acids can inhibit gelatinization.

    True   False

8. Once a cold emulsion sauce is prepared, you can keep it for several days under refrigeration.

    True   False

UNIT 4 ANSWER KEY

A. Terminology

All definitions can be found in the text.

B. Fill in the Blank

1. 32 degrees F (0 degrees C)
2. 450 degrees F (232 degrees C), 375 degrees F (191 degrees C)
3. acidity, or alkalinity
4. Metal
5. quickly, more rapidly
6. more slowly
7. emulsion
8. whipping again

C. Short Answer

1. Foods are dehydrated when water is removed by boiling it away, air-drying, or curing with salt.

2. Rehydration of foods occurs when water is introduced to dry foods by cooking or soaking them in it.

3. Fat; because it can stretch thin enough to capture small bubbles of air or gas

4. By stirring it as it cooks

5. By trapping moisture

6. a. Air
   b. Liquid
   c. Fat

7. Conduction carries the heat from the surface to the center.

8. By spreading throughout a food in such a way that it prevents proteins or carbohydrates from forming large groups or strings

D. Matching

1. f
2. b
3. g

4. h
5. i
6. e
7. j
8. a
9. c
10. d

E. True or False

1. True
2. True
3. False
4. False
5. False
6. True
7. True
8. True

UNIT 5
CULINARY MATH

A. Terminology: Fill in the blank space with the correct definition.

1. addition _____

2. multiplication _____

3. subtraction _____

4. division _____

5. equation _____

6. product _____

7. divisor _____

8. dividend _____

9. quotient _____

10. fraction _____

11. numerator _____

12. denominator _____

13. whole numbers _____

14. proper (or common) fraction _____

15. improper fraction _____

16. mixed numbers _____

17. ratio _____

18. decimals _____

19. percentages _____

20. yield percent _____

21. food cost percent _____

B. Fill in the Blank: Fill in the blank with the word that best completes the sentence.

1. When symbols are used to write out a problem, it is sometimes referred to as

   an _____.

2. The answer of a division problem is called the _____.

3. When we break something into pieces, each of those pieces represents a

   _____ of the original whole.

4. To turn an improper fraction into a whole or mixed number you

   _____ the denominator into the numerator.

5. In order to add or subtract fractions, you must give them a common

   _____.

6. When you multiply proper fractions, you multiply the

   _____ together to arrive at the numerator for the product.

7. When you multiply proper fractions, you multiply the

   _____ together to arrive at the denominator for the product.

8. The fraction 1/2 expressed as a ratio becomes _____ to

   _____.

9. The way that restaurants make money is to sell food for

   _____ than it costs to _____ the food.

10. If it takes 1 pound of carrots to produce 12 ounces of usable product, the yield

   percent would be _____.

C. Matching: Match each of the terms in List A with the appropriate response in List B.

List A	List B
___1. place values	a. 1-3/4
___2. answer in a division problem	b. 4/5
___3. 2 + 2 =	c. "part of a hundred"
___4. mixed number	d. 0.125
___5. proper fraction	e. ones, tens, hundreds
___6. improper fraction	f. quotient
___7. 1/8 converted to a decimal	g. addition equation
___8. percentage	h. 7/4

D. Multiple Choice: For each question, choose the one correct answer.

1. The two basic functions for combining numbers are:
   a. addition and subtraction
   b. addition and multiplication
   c. multiplication and division
   d. subtraction and division

2. Multiplication involves the multiplicand, the multiplier, and the:
   a. product
   b. dividend
   c. quotient
   d. divisor

3. In division, the number you divide into another number is referred to as the:
   a. dividend
   b. quotient
   c. divisor
   d. product

4. In order to divide fractions properly, the whole calculation is changed from division to:
   a. subtraction
   b. multiplication
   c. addition

31

5. A proper fraction can be converted to a decimal by:
    a. dividing the numerator into the denominator
    b. subtracting the numerator from the denominator
    c. dividing the denominator into the numerator
    d. subtracting the denominator from the numerator

6. The process a chef uses to determine the costs for each recipe is often referred to as:
    a. busy work
    b. yield percent
    c. costing out a recipe
    d. a profit statement

E. True or False: Circle either True or False to indicate the correct answer.

1. Whole numbers have a place value, which allows us to indicate a large number.

    True   False

2. When writing fractions, the numerator represents the part.

    True   False

3. When writing fractions, the denominator appears above, or just before a line.

    True   False

4. A whole number and a fraction together are referred to as a mixed number.

    True   False

5. When the numerator is smaller than the denominator, you have a proper fraction.

    True   False

6. When dividing fractions, it isn't necessary to convert mixed numbers to improper fractions before you begin.

    True   False

32

7. Ratios can be used to express the relationship of more than two elements.

        True   False

8. The numbers to the left of the decimal point are parts of a whole number.

        True   False

UNIT 5 ANSWER KEY

A. Terminology

   All definitions can be found in the text.

B. Fill in the Blank

   1. equation
   2. quotient
   3. fraction
   4. divide
   5. denominator
   6. numerators
   7. denominators
   8. 1 part to 2 parts
   9. more, produce
   10. 75%

C. Matching

   1. e
   2. f
   3. g
   4. a
   5. b
   6. h
   7. d
   8. c

D. Multiple Choice

   1. b
   2. a
   3. c
   4. b
   5. c
   6. c

E. True or False

   1. True
   2. True
   3. False

4. True
5. True
6. False
7. True
8. False

UNIT 6
RECIPES AND FOOD COST

A. Terminology: Fill in the blank space with the correct definition.

1. whole numbers _____

2. addition _____

3. multiplication _____

4. subtraction _____

5. division _____

6. equation _____

7. product _____

8. divisor _____

9. dividend _____

10. quotient _____

11. fraction _____

12. numerator _____

13. denominator _____

14. proper (or common) fraction _____

15. improper fraction _____

16. mixed numbers _____

17. ratio _____

18. decimals _____

19. percentages _____

20. yield percent _____

21. food cost percent _____

B. Short Answer: Provide a short response that correctly answers each question below.

1. List 3 ways that portion information can be expressed in a standardized recipe.

   a. _____

   b. _____

   c. _____

2. List 3 things the ingredient list in a standardized recipe might contain.

   a. _____

   b. _____

   c. _____

3. List 3 service items that might be included in a standardized recipe.

   a. _____

   b. _____

   c. _____

4. List 3 areas or steps in a standardized recipe that might affect your timing, and, therefore, need to be looked at carefully.

   a. _____

   b. _____

   c. _____

C. Common Units of Measure: Fill in the blanks for the following conversions.

1. 1 gallon = _____ quarts = _____ fluid oz.

2. 1 quart = _____ pints = _____ fluid oz.

3. 1 pint = _____ cups = _____ fluid oz.

4. 1 cup = _____ Tbs. = _____ fluid oz.

5. 1 Tbs. = _____ tsp. = _____ fluid oz.

6. 1 pound = _____ oz.

7. 3/4 pound = _____ oz.

8. 1/2 pound = _____ oz.

9. 1/4 pound = _____ oz.

10. 1 ounce = _____ fluid oz.

D. Recipe Conversion Factors: Fill in the blanks using the recipe conversion factor equation – Desired yield/original yield = RCF.

Note: Round all answers to the nearest hundredth decimal point.

1. The original recipe for mashed potatoes yields 7 lbs., but you only need 3 lbs.

   Conversion factor = _____

2. A recipe for creamed spinach yields 10 lbs. The chef calls for 18 lbs.

   Conversion factor = _____

3. A recipe for Basic French Dressing yields 2 qt. The chef requires 12 cups of dressing for a luncheon party.

   Conversion factor = _____

4. A recipe for brioche yields 6 lbs. You want to make 2 lbs.

   Conversion factor = _____

5. A recipe for Salsa Cruda yields 1 qt. You need 7 pints.

   Conversion factor = _____

6. The original recipe for coleslaw yields 25 portions, and you only need 10.

   Conversion factor = _____

7. The original recipe for minestrone soup yields 6 qt. The service instructions call for 24 8-oz. portions. Tonight the chef wants you to produce 15 qt.

   a. Conversion = _____
   b. How many portions will 15 qt. yield? _____

38

E. Cup Conversions: Convert the following cup measures to tablespoons and/or teaspoons.

1. 1 cup = _____ Tbs.

2. 3/4 cup = _____ Tbs.

3. 2/3 cup _____ Tbs. and _____ tsp.

4. 1/2 cup = _____ Tbs.

5. 1/3 cup = _____ Tbs. and _____ tsp.

6. 1/2 cup = _____ Tbs.

7. 1/8 cup = _____ Tbs.

8. 1 Tbs. = _____ tsp.

9. 1/2 Tbs. = _____ tsp.

F. Recipe Conversion

The original yield of the following recipe for Cream of Asparagus Soup was 6 quarts. The standardized recipe card calls for 24 portions of 8 oz. each. You want to serve 36 portions of 8 oz. each. Determine the conversion factor and convert the ingredient quantities. Convert the new yields back into quarts, pounds, cups, or ounces.

Ingredients: Old Yield	Conversion Factor	Ingredients: New Yield
6qt.	_____	_____
24 portions		_____
8 oz. each		_____
Chicken stock 4-1/2 qt.		_____
Asparagus 3 lbs.		_____
Onion 14 oz.		_____
Butter 9 oz.		_____

Flour	9 oz.	_____
Milk	1-1/2 qt.	_____
Heavy Cream	3 cups	_____

G. Calculating Unit Costs: Using the information given, calculate the unit cost of each ingredient.

1. One case of Number 10 canned tomatoes costs $30.00, and there are 6 cans per case. How much does one can cost? $ _____

2. One case of whole milk costs $13.50. Each case consists of (6) half-gallon containers.

   a. How much does each half-gallon cost? _____

   b. How much does one cup cost? _____

   c. How much does one ounce cost? _____

3. One case of (24) 6-oz. boneless, skinless chicken breasts costs $32.64. How much does each unit cost? $ _____

4. One case of seedless raisins weighing 20 pounds costs $33.80. How much is the cost per ounce of the raisins? $ _____

5. One case of table salt containing (12) 1 lb. units costs $11.76. What is the cost of each individual unit? $ _____

H. Calculating Cost Per Portion: Using the information given, calculate the cost per portion for each recipe.

1. The total cost of ingredients in a standardized clam chowder recipe is $23.28, and yields 24 servings. What is the cost of each serving? $ _____

2. The total cost for ingredients in a recipe for Gazpacho that yields 12 servings is $14.58. What is the cost per portion? $ _____

3. The ingredient cost for producing a roast beef banquet for 120 people includes: green salad: $97.00; dinner rolls: $41.00; roast beef: $397.00; carrots: $52.00; mashed potatoes: $39.00; ice cream: $98.00; coffee: $22.00. What is the cost to produce each meal? $ _____

4. Your restaurant purchases a beef tenderloin weighing 8.25 pounds and costing $57.66. The trim loss, after the chef prepares the tenderloin for portioning, is 2.75 pounds. The filets that will be cut from the remaining usable product will weigh 8 oz. each.

   a. What was the edible portion cost per pound of the tenderloin?

      $ _____

   b. How many steaks will be produced? _____

   c. What is the final portion cost for each steak? _____

I. True or False: Circle either True or False to indicate the correct answer.

   1. Recipes are meant to provide a list of ingredients and nothing more.

             True   False

   2. The desired yield is determined by multiplying the number of portions by the size of the individual portion.

             True   False

   3. Volume is a measurement of the space occupied by a solid, liquid, or gas.

             True   False

4. When using a container to hold a product as you weigh it, you need to account for the weight of that container by setting the tare weight.

     True   False

5. Olive oil is the only substance for which it can be safely assumed that 1 fluid ounce equals 1 ounce.

     True   False

6. Adding the approximate costs of each ingredient in your recipe will give you the total food cost for that recipe.

     True   False

7. Tournéing carrots is a good example of a preparation technique that will decrease the amount of trim loss.

     True   False

8. The edible portion represents the part of any ingredient that can be served to the guest.

     True   False

9. If all of an ingredient is used exactly as it was purchased, the as-purchased cost of that ingredient is exactly as it appears on the invoice.

     True   False

10. Finding additional uses for trim, although always a good idea, does not help to reduce overall costs.

     True   False

UNIT 6 ANSWER KEY

A. Terminology

All definitions can be found in the text.

B. Short Answer

1. a. Pieces per portion
   b. Weight per portion
   c. Volume per portion

2. a. The name and measurement of the ingredients needed
   b. Any advance preparation the ingredient requires
   c. Specify the ingredient variety or brand if necessary

3. a. Portioning information (if not already listed in the yield)
   b. Finishing and plating instructions
   c. Proper service temperatures

4. a. Ingredients that require advance preparation (stocks, basic sauces, or a marinade, for example) or that must be either heated or chilled
   b. Equipment that requires preparation (preheating a grill, assembling a meat grinder, conditioning a roasting pan)
   c. A resting period or an overnight cooling period (letting yeast doughs proof or gelatin-thickened foods gel, marinating foods, and so forth)

C. Common Units of Measure

1. 2 quarts, 128 fluid oz.
2. 2 pints, 32 fluid oz.
3. 2 cups, 16 fluid oz.
4. 16 Tbs., 8 fluid oz.
5. 3 tsp., 1/2 fluid oz.
6. 16 oz.
7. 12 oz.
8. 8 oz.
9. 4 oz.
10. 1/2 fluid oz.

D. Recipe Conversion Factors

1. .43
2. 1.8

3. 1.5
4. .33
5. 1.75
6. .4
7. a. 2.5
   b. 60

E. Cup Conversions

1. 16
2. 12
3. 10 and 2
4. 8
5. 5 and 1
6. 4
7. 2
8. 3
9. 1-1/2

F. Recipe Conversion

Conversion Factor	Ingredients: New Yield
1.5	36 portions
	8 oz. each
	288 oz. = 9 qt.

Chicken stock	6.75 qt.
Asparagus	4.5 lb.
Onion	18 oz.
Butter	13.5 oz.
Flour	13.5 oz.
Milk	2.25 qt.
Heavy Cream	4.5 cups

G. Calculating Unit Costs

1. $5.00
2. a. $2.25
   b. $.28
   c. $.04
3. $1.36
4. $.11
5. $.98

H. Calculating Cost Per Portion

    1. $.97
    2. $1.22
    3. $6.22
    4. a. $10.48
       b. 11
       c. $5.24

I. True or False

    1. False
    2. True
    3. True
    4. True
    5. False
    6. False
    7. False
    8. True
    9. True
    10. False

UNIT 7
EQUIPMENT IDENTIFICATION

A. Terminology: Fill in the blank space with the correct definition.

1. knives _____

2. hand tools _____

3. range _____

4. steamer _____

5. conventional ovens _____

6. induction ovens _____

7. microwave ovens _____

8. sieve _____

9. colander _____

10. cheesecloth _____

11. flat top range _____

12. ring tip _____

13. open burner range_____

14. convection steamer _____

15. induction cooktop _____

16. chafing dishes _____

B. Fill in the Blank: Fill in the blank with the word that best completes the sentence.

1. Ceramic blades are difficult to sharpen by hand because they are so

_____.

2. Hollow-ground blades are made by combining _____ sheets of metal, and have edges that are _____ or _____.

3. A utility knife is a lighter version of a _____ knife.

4. A _____ is used to hone a knife as you work.

5. Composition cutting boards are constructed from _____ materials.

6. Another name for a Parisienne scoop is a _____.

7. Balloon whips are designed to incorporate _____ for making _____.

8. Nested measuring cups are used for _____ and _____ ingredients.

9. The metal stem of a bi-metallic coil thermometer must be inserted about _____ inches into the food, and takes about _____ seconds to display an accurate reading.

10. Candy, jelly, and deep fat thermometers have _____ stems.

C. Short Answer: Provide a short response that correctly answers each question below.

1. List 2 reasons to use stainless steel pots and pans.

   a. _____

   b. _____

2. List 4 types of sieves or strainers used in the commercial kitchen, and give a brief description of each one.

   a. _____

   b. _____

   c. _____

   d. _____

3. List the 3 steps generally used for cleaning and shining copper cookware.

   a. _____

   b. _____

   c. _____

4. List the 2 major differences between a sauteuse and a sautoir.

   a. _____

   b. _____

5. List 3 safety precautions that should be observed when working with large equipment.

   a. _____

   b. _____

   c. _____

D. Matching: Match each of the pans for oven cooking in List A with their description or appropriate use in List B.

List A	List B
___1. roasting pan	a. rectangular pan, may be full, half, or quarter size
___2. roasting rack	b. have lids designed to produce square loaves

___3. braising pan lids   c. made in two pieces

___4. gratin dishes   d. have a removable bottom

___5. Pullman loaf pans   e. used for roasting and baking

___6. spring form pans   f. have small, round cups

___7. sheet pan   g. round pans with flared sides, typically one to two inches in height

___8. muffin tins   h. used to trap moisture and baste foods as they cook

___9. pie pans   i. holds foods as they cook so that all surfaces are properly heated

___10. loose-bottomed tart pans   j. shallow baking dish made of ceramic, enameled cast iron, or enameled steel

E. Multiple Choice: For each question, choose the one correct answer.

1. Another name for an immersion blender is:
    a. hand blender
    b. stick blender
    c. burr mixer
    d. all of the above

2. Flattop ranges:
    a. have a thick solid plate of cast iron or steel set over the heat source
    b. generate heat by means of the magnetic attraction between the cooktop and a steel or cast iron pan
    c. have open burners that may be electric elements or gas
    d. make it easy to adjust the heat level quickly

3. Convection ovens:
    a. normally consist of two to four decks, though single-deck models are available
    b. have fans that force hot air to circulate around the food, cooking it evenly and quickly
    c. treat foods with smoke and can be operated at either cool or hot temperatures
    d. generate microwave radiation, which cooks or reheats foods very quickly

4. When a three-compartment sink is used for washing tools and equipment:
   a. the first sink is filled with a sanitizer
   b. the first sink is filled with hot rinse water
   c. the second sink is filled with a sanitizer
   d. the second sink is filled with hot rinse water

5. To keep foods hot during service, you should use:
   a. a combination steamer oven
   b. a steam table
   c. a salamander
   d. tiered steamers

F. True or False: Circle either True or False to indicate the correct answer.

1. Instant-read thermometers should be used to monitor reach-in refrigeration units.

   True   False

2. Walk-in refrigeration units are never located outside the facility.

   True   False

3. Ware washing machines use either high temperature or chemicals to properly wash and sanitize tableware, glassware, and flatware.

   True   False

4. Insulated storage containers are only used to keep foods hot.

   True   False

5. Refrigerated drawers or under-counter reach-ins allow foods on the line to be held at the proper temperature.

   True   False

6. The bottom of a steam table is filled with a small amount of water and a heat source keeps the water hot.

   True   False

7. Sneeze guards may be required on salad bars to keep foods from becoming contaminated during self-service.

   True   False

8. Before placing any foods in a storage container, the container should be cleaned and foods should be at the appropriate temperature.

       True   False

9. Reach-ins are the largest style of refrigeration found in professional kitchens.

       True   False

10. Always use metal, not plastic containers, to hold foods (after they are properly cooled) in the refrigerator or freezer.

       True   False

UNIT 7 ANSWER KEY

A. Terminology

All definitions can be found in the text.

B. Fill in the Blank

1. hard
2. two, beveled, fluted
3. chef's
4. steel
5. man-made
6. melon baller
7. air, foams
8. dry, solid
9. two, fifteen
10. liquid-filled

C. Short Answer

1. a. Stainless steel is easy to maintain.
    b. Stainless steel will not react with food.

2. a. A food mill has a flat, curving blade that rotates over a disk and is turned by a hand-operated crank.
    b. A drum sieve (tamis) is a tinned-steel, nylon, or stainless-steel screen stretched in an aluminum or wood frame.
    c. A colander is a perforated stainless-steel or aluminum bowl, with or without a base.
    d. Cheesecloth is light, fine mesh gauze used to strain liquids and to make sachet bags.

3. a. Mix equal parts of flour and salt, and then add enough distilled white vinegar to form a paste.
    b. Coat copper surfaces completely with this paste, then vigorously massage clean with a cloth.
    c. Rinse with hot water and air dry completely before storing.

4. a. A sauteuse has sloping sides.
    b. A sautoir has straight sides.

5. a. Learn to use the machine safely by getting instruction and reading the manufacturer's instructions.
   b. Turn off and unplug electrical equipment before you take it apart or put it back together.
   c. Use all safety features: Be sure that lids are secure, hand guards are used, and the machine is stable.

D. Matching

1. e
2. i
3. h
4. j
5. b
6. c
7. a
8. f
9. g
10. d

E. Multiple Choice

1. a
2. a
3. b
4. d
5. b

F. True or False

1. False
2. False
3. True
4. False
5. True
6. True
7. True
8. True
9. False
10. False

UNIT 8
BASIC KNIFE SKILLS

A. Terminology: Fill in the blank space with the correct definition.

1. forged blade _____

2. stamped blade _____

3. taper ground edge _____

4. serrated edge _____

5. bolster _____

6. full tang _____

7. partial tang _____

8. rat-tail tang _____

9. rivets _____

10. sharpening _____

11. sharpening stone _____

12. grit _____

13. honing _____

14. steel _____

15. cutting surface _____

16. knife guards (or sheaths) _____

17. knife grip _____

18. chiffonade _____

19. rondelles _____

20. gaufrette _____

21. oblique _____

22. julienne _____

54

23. batonnet _____

24. brunoise _____

25. dice _____

26. tourné _____

27. parisienne _____

B. Short Answer: Provide a short response that correctly answers each question below.

   1. List 3 factors that are true of forged blades.

      a. _____

      b. _____

      c. _____

   2. List 3 factors that are true of stamped blades.

      a. _____

      b. _____

      c. _____

   3. List 3 materials that are used to make knife handles.

      a. _____

      b. _____

      c. _____

4. List 4 guidelines for honing a knife on steel.

a. _____

b. _____

c. _____

d. _____

C. Matching: Match each of the terms in List A with the appropriate measurement in List B.

List A	*List B*
___1. fine brunoise	a. 1/8 x 1/8 x 1 to 2 inches
___2. paysanne	b. 3/4 x 3/4 x 3/4 inch
___3. julienne	c. approximately 2 inches long with seven faces
___4. batonnet	d. 1/16 x 1/16 x 1/16 inch
___5. lozenge	e. 1/2 x 1/2 x 1/2 inch
___6. brunoise	f. 1/4 x 1/4 x 1/4 inch
___7. medium dice	g. 1/2 x 1/2 x 1/8 inch
___8. small dice	h. diamond shape, 1/2 x 1/2 x 1/8 inch
___9. large dice	i. 1/4 x 1/4 x 2 to 2-1/2 inches
___10. tourné	j. 1/8 x 1/8 x 1/8 inch

D. Multiple Choice: For each question, choose the one correct answer.

1. A knife with a serrated edge is often used for:
   a. dicing vegetables
   b. slicing foods with a crust or firm skin
   c. mincing garlic
   d. carving vegetables for garnishes

2. Wooden handles are attached to the blade with:
   a. glue
   b. welding
   c. rivets
   d. screws

3. When carrying an unsheathed knife in the kitchen, you should hold it:
   a. straight down at your side
   b. straight out in front of you
   c. behind your back
   d. up against your chest

4. The approximate angle that is usually recommended when sharpening a knife on a stone is:
   a. 10-degrees
   b. 30-degrees
   c. 5-degrees
   d. 20-degrees

5. When using a knife, the guiding hand:
   a. is the hand that isn't holding the knife
   b. keeps the food stable
   c. helps control the size and consistency of your cuts
   d. all of the above

6. Which of the following is *not* a requirement for your work station mise en place?
   a. a container of double-strength sanitizing solution
   b. clean wiping cloths
   c. a selection of knives, laid out on the counter
   d. side towels

7. When using the coarse stone to sharpen your knife, how many strokes should you make for each side of the blade before moving to the next finer grit?
   a. 20
   b. 5
   c. 25
   d. 10

8. The best way to hold a knife:
   a. depends on how tall you are
   b. depends on how strong you are
   c. depends on the particular task and the specific knife
   d. depends on the amount of experience you have in the kitchen

9. Tools for shredding and grating include all of the following except:
   a. a chef's knife
   b. a slicer
   c. a box grater
   d. a parisienne scoop

10. Brunoise comes from the French word *brunoir* which means:
    a. to brown
    b. to cut very small
    c. to garnish
    d. to mince

E. True or False: Circle either True or False to indicate the correct answer.

1. Forged blades are tempered to improve strength and durability.

   True   False

2. Knives that have a collar that looks like a bolster, but is actually a separate piece attached to the handle, should be avoided because they tend to come apart easily.

   True   False

3. Chefs prefer electric knife sharpeners because there is no danger of over-sharpening the blade.

   True   False

4. When sharpening your knife on a stone, the duller the blade, the coarser the grit should be.

   True   False

5. You should sanitize your knives by running them through the dishwasher.

   True   False

6. Color-coded cutting boards are used to help prevent cross-contamination.

   True   False

7. Slotted hangers for storing knives should be mounted on the side of prep tables.

   True   False

8. Cutting boards should be towel-dried to prevent moisture damage.

        True   False

9. The chiffonade cut is no different than shredding.

        True   False

10. The paysanne cut is a diamond shape.

        True   False

UNIT 8 ANSWER KEY

A. Terminology

All definitions can be found in the text.

B. Short Answer

1. a. They are tempered to improve strength and durability.
    b. They are made when heated metal rods or bars are dropped into a mold, and then struck with a hammer to pound it to the correct shape and thickness.
    c. They are typically more expensive than stamped blades.

2. a. They are made by cutting blade-shaped pieces from sheets of previously milled steel.
    b. The blades are of a uniform thickness.
    c. The blades may be lighter than some forged blades.

3. a. Hard woods such as walnut and rosewood
    b. Textured metal
    c. Composition materials (vinyl)

4. a. Allow yourself plenty of room as you work.
    b. Stand with your weight evenly distributed.
    c. Hold the steel with your thumb and fingers safely behind the guard.
    d. Keep the knife blade at a 20-degree angle to the steel.

C. Matching

1. d
2. g
3. a
4. i
5. h
6. j
7. e
8. f
9. b
10. c

D. Multiple Choice

1. b
2. c

3. a
4. d
5. d
6. c
7. d
8. c
9. d
10. a

E. True or False

1. True
2. True
3. False
4. True
5. False
6. True
7. False
8. False
9. False
10. False

UNIT 9
DAIRY, EGGS, AND DRY GOODS

A. Terminology: Fill in the blank space with the correct definition.

1. pasteurization _____

2. homogenization _____

3. fermented _____

4. cultured _____

5. fresh cheese _____

6. rind ripened cheese _____

7. semi-soft cheese _____

8. hard cheese _____

9. grating cheese _____

10. blue cheese _____

11. dry goods _____

12. aseptic packaging _____

13. converted rice _____

B. Fill in the Blank: Fill in the blank with the word that best completes the sentence.

1. Do not store milk, cream, or butter near foods with _____.

2. Milk, as it comes from the cow, contains fat, known as

   _____ or _____.

3. Sour cream is a cultured sweet cream with _____% milk

   fat.

4. Sherbet may contain eggs and/or milk, but does not contain

   _____.

5. The best-quality butter, labeled grade AA, is made from sweet cream and

   contains at least _____% fat.

6. Soft or rind-ripened cheeses ripen from the _____ to the

   _____.

7. Grains are the _____ and _____ of

   cereal grasses.

C. Matching: Match each of the terms in List A with the appropriate description in List B.

List A	*List B*
___1. milled grains	a. ground hominy, available in fine, medium, and coarse grinds
___2. flours	b. a blend of hard and soft wheat, finely milled
___3. cracked wheat	c. very finely milled rice; powdery and white with a mild flavor
___4. all-purpose flour	d. made from coarsely crushed, minimally processed kernels
___5. semolina	e. round, short grain rice, very starchy and sticky when cooked
___6. brown rice	f. polished to remove all or some of the germ, bran, and/or hull
___7. basmati rice	g. produced by milling grains into a fine powder
___8. sushi rice	h. extra-long grain rice with an aromatic flavor

___9. rice flour

i. milled from durum wheat, normally pale yellow

___10. grits

j. whole rice grain with the husk removed

D. Multiple Choice: For each question, choose the one correct answer.

1. Milk products are inoculated with a bacterial strain to:
   a. aid in pasteurization
   b. cause fermentation
   c. complete the homogenization process
   d. meet government standards for ice cream

2. Sorbets contain:
   a. no milk
   b. no less than 10% milk
   c. no more than 20% milk
   d. no more than 30% milk

3. The best grade butter is labeled:
   a. grade A
   b. grade AA
   c. grade AAA
   d. grade AAAA

4. Semi-soft cheeses:
   a. are not suitable for grating
   b. have a soft, velvety skin
   c. are ideal for slicing
   d. typically have a heavy wax rind

5. When a high quality egg is broken onto a plate:
   a. the white is thick and does not spread unduly
   b. the yolk is centered and rides high on the white
   c. the yolk is anchored in place by membranes known as the chalazae
   d. all of the above

6. Stone ground grains remain at a lower temperature during milling and:
   a. tend to retain more of their nutritive value
   b. tend to retain less of their nutritive value
   c. lose all of their nutritive value
   d. do not lose any of their nutritive value

E. True or False: Circle either True or False to indicate the correct answer.

1. Whole grains have been milled to remove all or some of the germ.

    True   False

2. Flours are produced by milling grains (as well as other starchy ingredients such as beans or nuts) into a fine powder.

    True   False

3. All-purpose flour is a blend of hard and soft wheat that is finely milled. It has an off-white color and may be enriched or bleached.

    True   False

4. Durum flour is low in protein and seldom used for breads or pastas.

    True   False

5. Converted or parboiled rice is soaked and steamed before the husk, bran, and germ are removed; grains are fluffy and stay separated when cooked.

    True   False

6. Cornstarch is made from dried corn kernels with the hull and germ removed. The kernels are ground to pure white powder.

    True   False

7. Dried beans or peas and lentils are the dried mature seeds of pod-vegetables.

    True   False

8. Both whole and ground spices retain their potency for about six months if properly stored.

    True   False

9. Toasting spices before grinding them intensifies the flavor of some spices.

    True   False

10. Black, white, and red peppercorns are from the same plant.

    True   False

UNIT 9 ANSWER KEY

A. Terminology

All definitions can be found in the text.

B. Fill in the Blank

1. strong odors
2. milk fat, butterfat
3. 18
4. cream
5. 80
6. outside, center
7. fruit, seed

C. Matching

1. f
2. g
3. d
4. b
5. i
6. j
7. h
8. e
9. c
10. a

D. Multiple Choice

1. b
2. a
3. b
4. c
5. a
6. a

E. True or False

1. False
2. True
3. True
4. False

5. True
6. True
7. True
8. False
9. True
10. False

UNIT 10
MEAT AND POULTRY IDENTIFICATION AND FABRICATION

A. Terminology: Fill in the blank space with the correct definition.

1. inspection _____

2. grading _____

3. yield grade _____

4. market forms _____

5. primal _____

6. subprimal _____

7. portion control _____

8. boxed meat _____

9. meat fabrication _____

10. trimming _____

11. silverskin _____

12. poultry _____

13. ratites _____

14. trussing _____

15. disjointing _____

B. Fill in the Blank: Fill in the blank with the word that best completes the sentence.

1. A ham can be a _____, _____ or

    _____ ham.

2. Pigs are commonly slaughtered under the age of _____

    months.

3. Common cooking methods for the Boston butt primal cuts include

_____, _____, and

_____.

4. Lamb becomes _____ as it ages and develops a

_____, _____ taste.

5. A lamb leg may be _____ to stuff or before grilling.

6. A rack of lamb is typically _____, and the bones may be

_____ before cooking.

7. Game meats sold in restaurants are _____ raised for food.

8. Most large game animals produce meat that is _____,

_____, and free from _____ fat.

9. _____ is the most common small game animal.

10. _____ is a tough membrane that surrounds some cuts of

meat, and gets its name from its _____ color.

C. Short Answer: Provide a short response that correctly answers each question below.

1. List 3 procedures used in removing surface fat from meats during the trimming process.

a. _____

b. _____

c. _____

2. List 4 steps in the procedure used when cutting and pounding meat cutlets or scallops.

   a. _____

   b. _____

   c. _____

   d. _____

3. List 3 things to check for when receiving meats.

   a. _____

   b. _____

   c. _____

4. List 4 steps to follow when grinding meats.

   a. _____

   b. _____

   c. _____

   d. _____

D. Matching: Match the poultry product in List A with its average appropriate weight in List B.

List A	List B
___1. Rock Cornish game hen	a. 8 to 22 lb.
___2. roaster	b. 1-1/2 to 2 lb.
___3. fryer	c. 3/4 to 1-1/2 lb.
___4. capon	d. 4 to 6 lb.
___5. broiler	e. under 1 lb.
___6. young hen or tom turkey	f. 3-1/2 to 5 lb.

___7. yearling turkey   g. 3/4 to 2 lb.

___8. squab   h. 2-1/2 to 3-1/2 lb.

___9. roaster duckling   i. 5 to 8 lb.

___10. Guinea hen or fowl   j. 10 to 30 lb.

E. Multiple Choice: For each question, choose the one correct answer.

1. The flavor, color, and texture of any meat is influenced by:
   a. the amount of exercise the muscle receives
   b. the type of feed the animal receives
   c. the breed of the animal
   d. all of the above

2. During processing, raw poultry must be chilled to:
   a. 32 degrees F
   b. 36 degrees F
   c. 41 degrees F
   d. 26 degrees F

3. The following USDA poultry grades are available except for:
   a. A
   b. AA
   c. B
   d. C

4. The object of trussing any bird is:
   a. so that it will cook evenly and retain moisture
   b. so that it will look better when served
   c. so that it will take less time to cook
   d. so that it will take more time to cook

5. Cutting into halves is an especially important technique for use on:
   a. capons and young hens
   b. roasters and yearling turkeys
   c. Cornish game hens and broiler chickens
   d. Roaster ducklings and goslings

F. True or False: Circle either True or False to indicate the correct answer.

1. Most meats are inspected by federal inspectors.

             True   False

2. Consumers pay for federal or state meat inspections.

   True   False

3. The grade placed on a particular carcass is then applied to all the cuts from that animal.

   True   False

4. The first cuts made in butchering a large animal are the subprimal cuts.

   True   False

5. Boxed meats are usually packed in Cryovac before shipping.

   True   False

6. The largest percentage of beef is graded prime.

   True   False

7. The most common cooking methods for cuts from the beef primal known as the round are sautéing and grilling.

   True   False

8. Moist heat methods such as stewing, simmering, and braising are appropriate for cuts from the chuck primal cuts of beef.

   True   False

9. Milk-fed veal comes from calves that have not been fed grass or feed for more than 12 weeks.

   True   False

10. The pork you buy may have quality grades assigned by the meat packer, rather than federal grades.

   True   False

UNIT 10 ANSWER KEY

A. Terminology

All definitions can be found in the text.

B. Fill in the Blank

1. fresh, cured, smoked
2. 12
3. roasting, sautéing, stewing
4. tougher, strong, gamey
5. butterflied
6. roasted, frenched
7. commercially
8. dark red, very lean, intramuscular
9. rabbit
10. silverskin, silvery

C. Short Answer

1. a. Hold the knife blade so that it is parallel to the lean meat.
   b. Make straight, smooth cuts to remove as much of the visible or surface fat as desired.
   c. Use the flat side of the knife blade to steady the meat as you lift and pull away the layer of fat.

2. a. Trim the meat completely, removing all visible fat, sinew, gristle, and silverskin.
   b. Cut pieces of about the same thickness and weight.
   c. Place the meat between two layers of plastic wrap.
   d. Use a pounding and pushing motion to evenly thin the cutlet.

3. a. Meats should be received at 41 degreesF (5degrees C).
   b. Look for packaging that is clean and intact.
   c. Check the temperature of the delivery truck.

4. a. Clean the grinder well and put it together correctly.
   b. Make sure that the blade is sitting flush against the die.
   c. Cut the meat into dice or strips that will fit easily through the grinder's feed tube.
   d. Continue to grind through progressively smaller dies until the desired consistency is achieved.

D. Matching

1. g
2. f
3. h
4. i
5. b
6. a
7. j
8. e
9. d
10. c

E. Multiple Choice

1. d
2. d
3. b
4. a
5. c

F. True or False

1. True
2. False
3. True
4. False
5. True
6. False
7. False
8. True
9. False
10. True

UNIT 11
FISH AND SHELLFISH IDENTIFICATION AND FABRICATION

A. Terminology: Fill in the blank space with the correct definition.

1. whole fish _____

2. drawn fish _____

3. dressed fish _____

4. fillet _____

5. low activity fish _____

6. medium activity fish _____

7. high activity fish _____

8. univalves _____

9. bivalves _____

10. crustaceans _____

11. cephalopods _____

12. shucked _____

13. count _____

14. pin bones _____

15. paupiette _____

16. goujonette _____

17. beard _____

B. Fill in the Blank: Fill in the blank with the word that best completes the sentence.

1. Shrimp that have been boiled or steamed in the shell are

_____ and _____ than shrimp that were

peeled and deveined before cooking.

2. When soft-shelled crabs are served, the shells are usually

   _____ along with the meat.

3. Unlike clams and oysters, _____ often have a dark, shaggy

   beard.

4. Frozen whole fish may be coated with water and frozen repeatedly to glaze

   the fish and protect it from _____ _____.

5. Fresh finfish should have _____ that are bright pink to

   maroon in color.

6. When storing drawn fish the belly cavity should be filled with

   _____ _____.

7. Frozen fish should be stored at _____.

8. Live or fresh shellfish are best stored at a temperature of between

   _____.

C. Matching: Match the type of fish or shellfish named in List A with its description
   in List B.

List A	*List B*
___1. low activity fish	a. have cartilage rather than bones
___2. medium activity fish	b. have a middle backbone and one fillet on either side of the backbone
___3. high activity fish	c. relatively dark flesh and pronounced flavors
___4. flat fish	d. delicate in flavor and texture

____5. round fish

                       e. their shell is usually eaten along with the meat

____6. nonbony fish

                       f. moderately fatty or oily

____7. mollusks

                       g. if its shell won't open, it's dead and should be discarded

____8. lobster

                       h. eyes on the same side of the head

____9. shrimp

                       i. contains tomalley and coral

____10. soft-shelled crabs

                       j. cleaned by removing their shell and the vein that runs along the back

D. Multiple Choice: For each question, choose the one correct answer.

1. When checking finfish for freshness, the eyes should be:
    a. clear, bright, and sunken
    b. clear, dull, and bulging
    c. clear, bright, and bulging
    d. clear, dull, and sunken

2. Under ideal conditions, the chef should purchase:
    a. enough fish to last a day or two
    b. enough fish to last three or four days
    c. enough fish to last four to five days
    d. enough fish to last one week

3. The color, flavor, and texture of fish is determined by:
    a. the water it lives in (warm or cold)
    b. the water it lives in (fresh or salt)
    c. how active the fish is
    d. all of the above

4. Low activity fish are typically prepared by:
    a. grilling
    b. pan-frying
    c. sautéing
    d. gentle moist heat cooking

5. Medium activity fish are suitable for:
    a. all cooking methods
    b. only deep-fat frying
    c. only grilling
    d. only moist-heat cooking

6. High activity fish are particularly suitable for:
   a. poaching
   b. simmering
   c. grilling
   d. steaming

7. Storing live shellfish in fresh ice water will:
   a. kill them
   b. prolong their shelf life
   c. lessen their shelf life
   d. have no affect on their shelf life

8. The most popular of all shellfish is:
   a. lobster
   b. crabs
   c. shrimp
   d. crayfish

9. Which of the following are cephalopods?
   a. shrimp and crayfish
   b. mussels and clams
   c. lobsters and crabs
   d. squid and octopus

10. The first step when preparing a lobster to boil or steam is:
    a. wash it
    b. kill it
    c. weigh it
    d. remove its claws

E. True or False: Circle either True or False to indicate the correct answer.

1. Drawn fish have the viscera removed, plus the head, fins, and scales.

        True   False

2. One sign of fresh fish is that the scales (if any) should tightly adhere to the fish.

        True   False

3. Fish and shellfish can be held for 6–7 days without losing any appreciable quality.

        True   False

4. To store fish fillets, lay the fillets directly on shaved ice.

    True   False

5. When referring to shellfish, shucking indicates that the seafood has been removed from the shell.

    True   False

6. Live or fresh shellfish are best stored at temperatures between 40 degrees and 50 degrees F/4.44 degrees C and 10 degrees C.

    True   False

7. Live crabs and lobsters should be packed in seaweed or damp paper upon delivery.

    True   False

8. Shucked shellfish delivered in containers should be stored in their containers, under refrigeration.

    True   False

9. A flat fish will yield two fillets, a round fish will yield four.

    True   False

10. A paupiette is a small, stuffed mollusk.

    True   False

UNIT 11 ANSWER KEY

A. Terminology

All definitions can be found in the text.

B. Fill in the Blank

1. moister, plumper
2. eaten
3. mussels
4. freezer burn
5. gills
6. flaked ice
7. –20 degrees F to 0 degrees F/–29 degrees C to –1 degree C
8. 35 degrees and 40 degrees F/1 degree C and 4 degrees C

C. Matching

1. d
2. f
3. c
4. h
5. b
6. a
7. g
8. i
9. j
10. e

D. Multiple Choice

1. c
2. a
3. d
4. d
5. a
6. c
7. a
8. c
9. d
10. b

E. True or False

1. False
2. True
3. False
4. False
5. True
6. False
7. True
8. True
9. False
10. False

UNIT 12
FRESH PRODUCE: FRUITS, VEGETABLES, AND FRESH HERBS

A. Terminology: Fill in the blank space with the correct definition.

1. produce _____

2. ethylene gas _____

3. local, seasonal foods _____

4. boutique farmers _____

5. specialty growers _____

6. foragers _____

7. artisan producers _____

8. fruits _____

9. individually quick frozen (IQF) _____

_____

10. freestone _____

11. clingstone _____

12. exotic _____

13. bitter salad greens _____

14. cooking greens _____

15. cultivated mushroom _____

16. tubers _____

17. herbs _____

18. concassé _____

19. plumped _____

B. Fill in the Blank: Fill in the blank with the word that best completes the sentence.

1. _____ is a good indicator of quality in both fresh and dried herbs.

2. Store herbs loosely wrapped in damp _____ and keep them _____.

3. Wash vegetables and herbs _____ any initial trim work is done.

4. _____ all cutting and work surfaces when you switch from one food item to another.

5. Once cut, garlic starts to take on a _____ flavor.

6. The flavor of garlic becomes rich, sweet, and smoky after _____.

7. One of the biggest concerns when working with leeks is removing all traces of _____.

8. Tomato concassé is prepared from whole tomatoes that are _____ and _____ before they are chopped.

9. Chiles retain a good deal of their heat in the _____, _____, and _____ ends.

10. Cook mushrooms as soon as possible after they are _____

for the best flavor, color, and consistency in the finished dish.

C. Short Answer: Provide a short response that correctly answers each question below.

1. List 3 guidelines for storing fresh produce.

   a. _____

   _____

   b. _____

   _____

   c. _____

   _____

2. List and describe 3 varieties of apples.

   a. _____

   _____

   b. _____

   _____

   c. _____

   _____

3. List and describe 3 berries.

   a. _____

   _____

   b. _____

   _____

c. _____

_____

D. Matching: Match each of the fruits in List A with the appropriate description in List B.

List A	*List B*
___1. Golden Delicious apples	a. pear-shaped with green to black leathery skin
___2. Northern Spy apples	b. includes Persian, Casaba, and Crenshaw; have a sweet scent when ripe
___3. blackberries	c. have a long neck, squat bottom with dark, russeted skin
___4. currants	d. have a blue-black, thick skin that slips easily from the flesh
___5. Concord grapes	e. have red skin, streaked with yellow
___6. Red Emperor grapes	f. large, purplish black fruits, similar in shape to raspberries
___7. honeydew-type melons	g. have yellowish skin with freckling
___8. Bosc pears	h. light to deep red with green streaking, their skin is thin and adheres tightly to the flesh
___9. apricots	i. tiny, round, smooth berries that may be white, red, or black
___10. avocados	j. smaller than peaches, with golden or orange flesh

E. Multiple Choice: For each question, choose the one correct answer.

1. Savoy, Napa, and bok choy are all types of:
   a. cabbage
   b. fruit
   c. tubers
   d. squash

2. Hard shell squashes are:
   a. stored under refrigeration
   b. members of the gourd family
   c. stored in bright, warm areas
   d. popular because their rinds are edible

3. Bitter salad greens are:
   a. leafy vegetables
   b. tender enough to be eaten in salads
   c. suitable to sauté or braise
   d. all of the above

4. Cultivated mushroom varieties include:
   a. cèpes
   b. cremini
   c. morels
   d. truffles

5. Green onions include:
   a. scallions
   b. garlic
   c. shallots
   d. pearl onions

6. When handling hot chiles, always:
   a. hold them under running water
   b. handle only with your bare hands
   c. avoid touching your eyes
   d. take no special precautions

7. Sugar snap peas, green beans, and wax beans are:
   a. picked when the pod is still fleshy and tender enough to eat
   b. removed from their inedible pods before eating
   c. best eaten when mature, not young
   d. picked when their pods begin to wilt and pucker

8. Jerusalem artichokes, sweet potatoes, and yams are all:
   a. root vegetables
   b. pod and seed vegetables
   c. shoot and stalks vegetables
   d. tubers

F. True or False: Circle either True or False to indicate the correct answer.

1. Keeping a kitchen properly stocked with fresh, high quality produce is one of the greatest challenges a chef faces.

                    True   False

2. Store fruits and vegetables that need further ripening, notably peaches and avocados, under refrigeration.

        True   False

3. Onions, garlic, lemons, and melons are among the fruits that give off odors that can permeate other foods.

        True   False

4. Fruits are the ovaries of a plant that surrounds or contains the seeds of the plant.

        True   False

5. Cooking varieties of apples are considered best for pies and baking; they tend to hold their shape when baked.

        True   False

6. Fresh berries are extremely perishable (with the exception of cranberries); they are susceptible to bruising, mold, and over-ripening.

        True   False

7. Bitter citrus is typically used to produce juices or marmalades; this group includes tangerines, mandarins, and tangelos.

        True   False

8. Serve grapes well chilled for the fullest flavor.

        True   False

UNIT 12 ANSWER KEY

A. Terminology

All definitions can be found in the text.

B. Fill in the Blank

1. aroma
2. paper towels, refrigerated
3. before
4. sanitize
5. stronger
6. roasting
7. dirt
8. peeled, seeded
9. seeds, ribs, blossom ends
10. cut

C. Short Answer

1. a. Storage temperatures for fresh produce should be maintained at 40 degrees F/4 degrees to 7 degrees C, with a relative humidity of 80 to 90 percent.
   b. The ideal situation is to have a separate walk-in or reach-in refrigerator reserved for fruits and vegetables.
   c. Keep fruits and vegetables dry; excess moisture promotes spoilage.

2. a. Golden Delicious apples have yellowish-green skin with freckling; they are crisp, juicy, and sweet, and are good all-purpose apples.
   b. Granny Smith apples have bright green skin. The flesh is white, crisp, and finely textured with a tart flavor. Granny Smiths are good all-purpose apples.
   c. Macintosh apples are primarily red with yellow or green streaks. The flesh is crisp, very juicy, and somewhat tart in flavor. Macintosh apples are good for eating out of hand or to cook into purees and sauces.

3. a. Blackberries are large, purplish black fruits, similar in shape to raspberries.
   b. Blueberries are small to medium round berries with bluish-purple, smooth skin.
   c. Cranberries are small, shiny, red berries. They are hard, dry, and sour; cranberries are usually cooked before eating.

D. Matching

    1. g
    2. e
    3. f
    4. i
    5. d
    6. h
    7. b
    8. c
    9. j
    10. a

E. Multiple Choice

    1. a
    2. b
    3. d
    4. b
    5. a
    6. c
    7. a
    8. d

F. True or False

    1. True
    2. False
    3. True
    4. True
    5. False
    6. True
    7. False
    8. False

UNIT 13
BASIC MISE EN PLACE

A. Terminology: Fill in the blank space with the correct definition.

1. aromatics _____

2. mise en place _____

3. bouquet garni _____

4. sachet d'épices _____

5. mirepoix _____

6. clarified butter _____

7. roux _____

8. slurry _____

9. liaison _____

10. tempering _____

11. beurre manié _____

12. oignon piqué _____

13. oignon brûlé _____

B. Fill in the Blank: Fill in the blank with the word that best completes the sentence.

1. When preparing a mirepoix, the vegetables should be thoroughly

   _____ and _____.

2. Mirepoix vegetables should be cut into pieces of a relatively

   _____ size.

3. Slice mirepoix _____ or _____ for

   fumets and stocks that simmer less than 1 hour.

4. Standard mirepoix is used for a variety of _____ and

   _____.

5. A matignon includes _____, _____,

   _____, and _____ cut into very neat

   dice.

6. Battuto includes _____ or chopped

   _____, _____, or

   _____, with _____,

   _____, _____, _____,

   _____, and/or _____.

7. When creating a pinçage, the heat is _____ to encourage

   even browning and avoid scorching.

8. Clarified butter is made by heating whole butter until the

   _____ and _____

   _____ separate.

9. The three basic colors of roux are _____,

   _____, and _____.

10. _____ roux has more thickening power than a

    _____ roux.

C. Matching: Match each of the terms in List A with the appropriate description in List B.

List A	*List B*
___1. bouquet garni	a. a French term for kneaded butter
___2. matignon	b. fresh herbs and vegetables, tied into a bundle
___3. Cajun trinity	c. has a strong, nutty aroma
___4. ghee	d. a peeled onion, cut crosswise and charred on the cut edges
___5. brown or dark roux	e. added to dishes as both a flavoring and as a garnish
___6. slurries	f. a bay leaf, fastened to an onion with a whole clove
___7. beurre manié	g. pure starches dissolved in a cold liquid
___8. liaison	h. onions, celery, and green pepper
___9. oignon piqué	i. a type of clarified butter
___10. oignon brûlé	j. a mixture of eggs and cream used to add body and sheen to a dish

D. Multiple Choice: For each question, choose the one correct answer.

1. Mise en place is a French phrase which means:
   a. everything out of place
   b. put in place
   c. put in motion
   d. start preparing right now

2. A bouquet garni is made up of fresh herbs and vegetables:
   a. tied in a bundle
   b. sprinkled over a roast
   c. added to a table setting
   d. none of the above

3. For less than a gallon of liquid, add the sachet or bouquet in the last:
   a. 5 minutes
   b. 15 minutes
   c. 45 minutes
   d. 60 minutes

4. Mirepoix and similar combinations provide:
   a. an intense flavor boost
   b. thickening power to a liquid
   c. a subtle background flavor
   d. a method of garnishing a soup

5. Battuto is used in:
   a. Cajun cuisine
   b. French style cooking
   c. Native American cuisine
   d. Italian soups, sauces, and stews

6. Cooking aromatic vegetables and other ingredients until they have a rich brown color and a robust, sweet flavor is known as:
   a. sweating
   b. smothering
   c. pinçage
   d. clarifying

7. Ghee, which is used in some Asian cuisines, is a:
   a. type of clarified butter
   b. type of aromatic vegetable
   c. type of thickening agent
   d. type of preservative

8. One pound of whole butter yields approximately _____ ounces of clarified butter.
   a. 8
   b. 10
   c. 12
   d. 14

9. The most common fat used to make roux is:
   a. vegetable oil
   b. olive oil
   c. sesame oil
   d. clarified butter

10. Just before a slurry is used it should be:
   a. heated to make it dissolve faster
   b. stirred to recombine the starch evenly
   c. seasoned
   d. strained

E. True or False: Circle either True or False to indicate the correct answer.

1. At its most basic, mise en place is about understanding your work.

          True   False

2. A bouquet garni sachet d'épices adds flavors to stocks, sauces, and soups by gently infusing the liquid with its aroma.

          True   False

3. A standard bouquet or sachet should never be modified by adding other ingredients.

          True   False

4. Mirepoix is the French name for a combination of onions, carrots, and celery.

          True   False

5. One pound of mirepoix is enough to flavor 3 gallons of stock, soup, sauce, stew, braise, or marinade.

          True   False

6. The French term, pinçage, refers to the browning of a mirepoix.

          True   False

7. When clarifying butter, salted butter is recommended because further seasoning will not be necessary.

          True   False

8. Roux thickens sauces, soups, and stews, as well as lending those dishes a special flavor.

          True   False

9. Vegetable oil is the most common fat used for making roux.

          True   False

10. The basic ratio (by weight) for a roux is 2 parts flour to 1 part fat.

          True   False

UNIT 13 ANSWER KEY

A. Terminology

All definitions can be found in the text.

B. Fill in the Blank

1. rinsed, trimmed
2. uniform
3. very fine, chop fine
4. stocks, soups
5. onions, carrots, celery, ham
6. olive oil, lard, pancetta, fatback, garlic, onions, parsley, carrots, celery, green peppers
7. adjusted
8. butterfat, milk solids
9. white, blond, brown
10. white, darker

C. Matching

1. b
2. e
3. h
4. i
5. c
6. g
7. a
8. j
9. f
10. d

D. Multiple Choice

1. b
2. a
3. b
4. c
5. d
6. c
7. a
8. c
9. d
10. b

E. True or False

1. True
2. True
3. False
4. True
5. False
6. True
7. False
8. True
9. False
10. False

UNIT 14
STOCKS

A. Terminology: Fill in the blank space with the correct definition.

1. stocks _____

2. basic stock or simple stock _____

3. white stock _____

4. blanching _____

5. neutral stocks _____

6. brown stocks _____

7. fumet _____

8. smothering _____

9. collagen _____

10. gelatin _____

11. rémouillage _____

12. dépouillage_____

13. meat glaze (or glaçe de viande) _____

_____

14. court bouillon _____

B. Fill in the Blank: Fill in the blank with the word that best completes the sentence.

1. For a rich, flavorful stock, the best bones to use should be very

_____ and taken from the joints (knuckle or hock) or the

neck.

2. Lean, white-fleshed fish; flatfish are the most common choice for

   _____ _____ or

   _____.

3. Standard flavoring preparations for stock include _____

   _____, _____ _____,

   _____, _____, and

   _____ _____.

4. A small amount of _____ is helpful to extract protein from

   the bones and make a richer stock.

5. The liquid for stock making should be _____ when they are

   combined with the main ingredients.

6. When preparing aromatic ingredients for stocks, the longer the stock simmers,

   the _____ the cuts can be.

7. The larger and denser the bones, the _____ the simmering

   time.

8. Longer simmering will reduce the water in the stock, reducing and

   concentrating the flavor and increasing the stock's _____.

9. Add flavoring ingredients such as mirepoix or a sachet d'épices when the

   stock has _____ minutes to _____

   _____ left to simmer.

10. After the stock is done simmering, you must _____ it from

the solid ingredients.

C. Short Answer: Provide a short response that correctly answers each question below.

1. List 3 guidelines for producing quality stocks.

   a. _____

   b. _____

   c. _____

2. List 3 examples of simple stocks.

   a. _____

   b. _____

   c. _____

3. List 2 reasons why the right size and shape stockpot helps assure a well-made stock.

   a. _____

   b. _____

4. List 4 tools you will need for correctly straining a stock that has finished simmering.

   a. _____

   b. _____

   c. _____

   d. _____

D. Multiple Choice: For each question, choose the one correct answer.

1. Glaçe de canard is made from _____ stock.
   a. chicken
   b. veal
   c. duck
   d. fish

2. Court bouillon is also known as a:
   a. short broth
   b. neutral stock
   c. fumet
   d. meat glaze

3. Commercially prepared bases are:
   a. used in place of stocks
   b. available in highly reduced forms
   c. helpful to deepen and improve a stock's flavor
   d. all of the above

4. Blanching bones for a white stock is typically done:
   a. to improve the flavor of the stock
   b. to improve the color of the stock
   c. when the bones have been frozen
   d. when the bones are not fresh

5. To further enhance the color and flavor of brown stocks, some chefs add:
   a. food coloring
   b. an oignon brûlée
   c. a sachet bag
   d. collagen

6. Shellfish stocks, made from lobster, shrimp, or crayfish shells, are made using the same basic technique as:
   a. a brown stock
   b. a basic stock
   c. a white stock
   d. a fumet

7. A fumet is typically made from:
   a. chicken bones
   b. shellfish bodies
   c. water and seasonings
   d. the bones of lean white flat fish

8. A stockpot should hold the ingredients for the stock, including the liquid, with at least _____ _____ of space at the top of the pot.
   a. two inches
   b. three inches
   c. four inches
   d. six inches

9. All vegetables, whether used as aromatics or as the main flavoring ingredient, must be _____ before being used.
   a. rinsed
   b. peeled
   c. crushed
   d. minced

10. The flavor of a finished stock should reflect:
   a. the seasonings used
   b. the method used
   c. the main ingredient
   d. the temperature at which it was cooked

E. True or False: Circle either True or False to indicate the correct answer.

1. White stocks are nearly colorless when they are heated.

   True   False

2. Stocks made from meat, poultry, game bones, or shells are seldom clear.

   True   False

3. Aroma and flavor in stocks is not as important as appearance.

   True   False

4. Brown stocks have a more pronounced, richer flavor than white stocks.

   True   False

5. A well made stock will have a rich texture or mouthfeel to it because of its seasonings.

   True   False

6. Blanching bones darkens the color and enriches the flavor of the stock.

   True   False

7. Quick-cooking stocks such as fish stock or fumet and vegetable stock benefit from the flavor boost they get when the main ingredients are gently cooked in some fat before the liquid is added.

        True   False

8. When a stock is finished simmering, it should be strained into a plastic container.

        True   False

9. Broths are essentially the same as stocks except that they are made with more meat than bones.

        True   False

10. To prepare a rémouillage, the bones and mirepoix from a stock are combined with fresh water and simmered.

        True   False

11. To prepare a glaçe, put the stock or rémouillage in a heavy gauge pan and simmer until it has reduced by about half.

        True   False

UNIT 14 ANSWER KEY

A. Terminology

All definitions can be found in the text.

B. Fill in the Blank

1. meaty
2. fish stocks, fumet
3. sachet d'épices, bouquet garni, mirepoix, tomato, and oignon brûlée.
4. salt
5. cold
6. larger
7. longer
8. body
9. 45, one hour
10. separate

C. Short Answer

1. a. Choose the best quality ingredients for the preparation.
   b. Use good technique, observing all standards for ingredient preparation, appropriate equipment, cooking temperatures, and flavor development.
   c. Evaluate what you have produced and judge it according to standard criteria for quality: appearance, flavor and aroma, and body.

2. a. Chicken stock
   b. Vegetable stock
   c. Fish stock

3. a. The stock has a smaller surface area, which helps to better extract flavor from the ingredients into the liquid.
   b. It encourages convection. This motion in the simmering stock brings impurities to the surface where thay can be skimmed away more easily.

4. a. Cheesecloth to line a sieve or colander
   b. Ladles to lift the stock away from the solid ingredients
   c. Equipment for cooling stocks
   c. Containers with lids to hold chilled stock

D. Multiple Choice

1. c
2. a

3. d
4. c
5. b
6. a
7. d
8. b
9. a
10. c

E. True or False

1. True
2. False
3. False
4. True
5. False
6. True
7. False
8. True
9. True
10. True

UNIT 15
SAUCES

A. Terminology: Fill in the blank space with the correct definition.

1. béchamel _____

2. beurre blanc _____

3. brown sauce _____

4. demi glace _____

5. emulsion sauces _____

6. espagnole sauce _____

7. grand sauce _____

8. hollandaise sauce _____

9. jus de veau lié _____

10. monter au beurre _____

11. reductions _____

12. tomato sauces _____

13. velouté _____

14. warm butter sauces _____

B. Fill in the Blank: Fill in the blank with the word that best completes the sentence.

1. White sauces scorch easily if they are not tended and can take on a grayish

    cast if prepared in _____.

2. To thicken 1 gallon of white sauce to a light consistency, you would need

    _____ ounces of blond or white roux.

3. Any sauce thickened with a _____ is susceptible to scorching.

4. An excellent white sauce should have a pale color, with absolutely no hint of _____.

5. White sauces are often finished with _____.

6. Escoffier's tomato sauce relied on _____ as a thickener.

7. If a tomato sauce is to be pureed, a _____ is typically used.

8. Hollandaise sauce is prepared by emulsifying melted or clarified butter and water (in the form of an acidic reduction and/or lemon juice) with partially cooked _____.

9. The success or failure of a hollandaise sauce depends on skillfully combining _____, _____, _____, and _____, and also on the quality of the _____ itself.

10. As the volume of hollandaise sauce increases, the amount of butter that can be emulsified with 1 egg yolk _____.

C. Short Answer: Provide a short response that correctly answers each of the questions below.

1. List the 5 steps in making a brown sauce.

a. _____

b. _____

c. _____

d. _____

e. _____

2. List the 7 steps in making a white sauce.

   a. _____

   b. _____

   c. _____

   d. _____

   e. _____

   f. _____

   g. _____

3. List the 5 steps in making a tomato sauce.

   a. _____

   b. _____

   c. _____

   d. _____

   e. _____

4. List the 6 steps in making hollandaise sauce.

   a. _____

   b. _____

   c. _____

d. _____

e. _____

f. _____

D. Matching: Match each of the terms in List A with the appropriate description in List B.

List A	*List B*
___1. espagnole sauce	a. cuisson
___2. jus lies	b. Romas
___3. monter au beurre	c. warm butter sauce
___4. classic velouté	d. prepared by bolstering a brown stock with additional aromatics and thickening it with roux
___5. plum tomatoes	e. emulsion sauce
___6. hollandaise sauce	f. finishing with butter
___7. shallow-poaching cooking liquid	g. "velvety, soft, and smooth to the pallet"
___8. beurre blanc	h. made by reducing brown stocks and thickening them with a pure starch slurry

E. Multiple Choice: For each question, choose the one correct answer.

1. The term *grand sauce* refers to a classic system of sauces based upon _____ culinary standards.
   a. Italian
   b. French
   c. American
   d. Modern

2. Espagnole sauce is prepared by bolstering a brown stock with additional aromatics and thickening it with:
   a. a pure starch slurry
   b. roux
   c. reduction
   d. Monter Au Beurre

3. Demi glaçe is made by combining equal parts of espagnole and brown stock and:
   a. thickening with roux
   b. adding a fortified wine
   c. reducing by half
   d. adding reduced heavy cream

4. Brown sauces are typically prepared in a saucepan or pot that:
   a. has a non-stick surface
   b. has a thin bottom
   c. is taller than it is wide
   d. is wider than it is tall

5. Brown sauces sometimes develop a skin when they are:
   a. held uncovered
   b. held covered
   c. held too long
   d. held at too high a temperature

6. The texture and, to some extent, the color of a brown sauce depends on the:
   a. type of pot used
   b. type of thickener used
   c. type of bones used
   d. type of stock used

7. When finishing a brown sauce, Port, Madeira, Marsala, or sherry is often blended into the simmering sauce:
   a. at the beginning of production
   b. half way through production
   c. just before serving
   d. after the sauce has cooled

8. The white sauce family includes the classic sauces velouté and béchamel, both produced:
   a. by thickening a liquid with a slurry
   b. by thickening a liquid by reduction
   c. by thickening a liquid with a liaison
   d. by thickening a liquid with roux

F. True or False: Circle either True or False to indicate the correct answer.

1. Only clarified butter can be used to make hollandaise sauce.

    True   False

2. For hollandaise sauce to come together successfully, the butter must be quite warm.

        True   False

3. A standard reduction for hollandaise consists of dry white wine, white wine vinegar, minced garlic, and fresh tarragon, reduced by half.

        True   False

4. When making hollandaise, the egg yolks should be whisked over boiling water until thickened and hot.

        True   False

5. When making hollandaise, the process of adding the butter to the egg yolks should be accomplished as fast as possible.

        True   False

6. Some hollandaise-style sauces are finished with minced herbs.

        True   False

7. The predominant flavor and aroma of a good hollandaise sauce is that of butter.

        True   False

8. Hollandaise should be a lemon-yellow color with a grainy texture.

        True   False

9. A standard reduction for a beurre blanc is made from dry white wine and shallots.

        True   False

10. The quality of the butter is not a critical factor to the success of a beurre blanc.

        True   False

UNIT 15 ANSWER KEY

A. Terminology

   All definitions can be found in the text.

B. Fill in the Blank

   a. an aluminum pan
   b. 10 to 12
   c. roux
   d. gray
   e. cream
   f. roux
   g. food mill
   h. egg yolks
   i. egg yolks, water, acid, butter, butter
   j. also increases

C. Short Answer

   1. a. Brown the trim and/or bones and mirepoix.
      b. Add the tomato paste and cook out until rust-colored.
      c. Add the brown stock to the bones and/or trim and mirepoix and simmer for 2 to 4 hours, skimming as necessary throughout the cooking time.
      d. Strain the sauce and finish as desired and hold at 165 degrees F/73 degrees C for service.
      e. Evaluate the quality of the finished brown sauce.

   2. a. Sweat the appropriate aromatics in fat.
      b. (Optional) Add the flour and cook, stirring frequently.
      c. Add the liquid to the roux gradually. Add sachet d'épices or bouquet garni, if desired.
      d. Add other seasoning or aromatics and simmer for 30 minutes to 1 hour stirring frequently and tasting throughout the cooking time.
      e. Strain the sauce.
      f. Finish as desired and hold at 165 degrees F (73 degrees C) for service.
      g. Evaluate the quality of the finished white sauce.

   3. a. Sweat or sauté the aromatic vegetables
      b. Add the tomatoes and any remaining ingredients and simmer until the flavor is fully developed, stirring frequently, skimming, and tasting throughout the cooking time.
      c. Purée the sauce if desired.
      d. Finish as desired.
      e. Evaluate the quality of the finished tomato sauce.

4. a. Make the reduction.
   b. Add the egg yolks to the reduction and whisk over barely simmering water until thickened and warm.
   c. Gradually whisk in the warm butter.
   d. Season to taste.
   e. Evaluate the quality of the finished hollandaise.
   f. Serve immediately or hold at or near 145 degrees F/63 degrees C for no more than 2 hours.

D. Matching

   1. d
   2. h
   3. f
   4. g
   5. b
   6. e
   7. a
   8. c

E. Multiple Choice

   1. b
   2. b
   3. c
   4. d
   5. a
   6. b
   7. c
   8. d

F. True or False

   1. False
   2. True
   3. False
   4. False
   5. False
   6. True
   7. True
   8. False
   9. True
   10. False

UNIT 16
SOUPS

A. Terminology: Fill in the blank space with the correct definition.

1. broth _____

2. consommé _____

3. clarification _____

4. puree soup _____

5. cream soup _____

6. bisque _____

7. garnish _____

8. ethnic or regional soups _____

B. Short Answer: Provide a short response that correctly answers each of the questions below.

1. List 3 types of soup and describe how they are made.

a. _____

_____

b. _____

_____

c. _____

_____

2. List 3 types of ethnic or regional soups and describe how they are made.

   a. _____

   _____

   b. _____

   _____

   c. _____

   _____

3. List the 5 steps in preparing a broth.

   a. _____

   _____

   b. _____

   _____

   c. _____

   _____

   d. _____

   _____

   e. _____

   _____

4. List 4 pieces of equipment you will need when making a consommé.

   a. _____

   b. _____

   c. _____

   d. _____

C. Matching: Match the soup or technique in List A with the appropriate description in List B.

List A	*List B*
___1. broths	a. invariable contain potatoes
___2. consommé	b. increase the quantity of beef from 8 pounds to 12 to 16 pounds
___3. minestrone, pepperpot, potage pistou	c. made from the stock of sautéed seafood shells
___4. purées	d. rice flour used to thicken
___5. cream soups	e. includes beans, pasta, and grated cheese
___6. bisques	f. a crystal clear soup
___7. minestrone	g. a clear liquid soup
___8. chowders	h. regional or ethnic specialty soup
___9. contemporary bisque	i. base may be a béchamel or velouté sauce
___10. double broth	j. consistency described as similar to a pancake batter

D. Multiple Choice: For each question, choose the one correct answer.

1. The classic approach to preparing a cream soup calls for:
   a. a clarification
   b. the main ingredient to be simmered in a velouté or béchamel sauce
   c. keeping the main ingredient firm
   d. producing a soup that has a chunky texture

2. Equipment needed to prepare a cream soup include:
   a. a colander
   b. a fine sieve or cheesecloth
   c. a bowl and whisk
   d. all of the above

3. Any soup can scorch if you:
   a. leave it unattended as it cooks
   b. use a flame diffuser
   c. stir the soup as it cooks
   d. use a flat top range

4. The term bisque is derived from:
   a. the use pure starch as a thickener
   b. the use of pureed lobster shells as a thickener
   c. the use of dry bread as a thickener
   d. the use of roux as a thickener

5. Which of the following is used to give a bisque flavor and color?
   a. tomato paste
   b. onion brûlée
   c. sachet
   d. potatoes

6. To check the flavor and quality of a stock you should:
   a. taste it when it's cold
   b. smell it
   c. bring it to a boil
   d. look at its clarity

7. Soups should be seasoned:
   a. throughout the cooking process
   b. only at the end of the cooking process
   c. only at the beginning of the cooking process
   d. only in the middle of the cooking process

8. As a general rule, cream soups and bisques should be as thick as:
   a. consommé
   b. cold heavy cream
   c. tomato sauce
   d. sour cream

9. To thin a soup that is too thick:
   a. add heavy cream
   b. add broth or water
   c. allow to simmer for 10 minutes
   d. allow to simmer for 20 minutes

10. To adequately address both quality and food safety concerns, soup should be held at a temperature of:
   a. 140 degrees F
   b. 150 degrees F
   c. 165 degrees F
   d. 180 degrees F

E. True or False: Circle either True or False to indicate the correct answer.

1. Some bisques are based upon vegetables, such as tomatoes.

   True   False

2. Once a broth has begun to simmer, no other ingredients should be added.

    True   False

3. The best time to taste a soup for quality and flavor is after it has finished simmering.

    True   False

4. Final seasoning and flavor adjustments of soups are generally done after the major flavoring ingredients have given up the maximum flavor and right before service.

    True   False

5. For a consommé, choose a meat high in fat content, that complements the flavor of the broth or that will add a specific flavor of its own.

    True   False

6. When making consommé, once the raft forms, adjust the heat until only a few small bubbles break the surface.

    True   False

7. If the first clarification of a consommé was less than successful, a second clarification is not possible.

    True   False

8. Vegetable soups are never made by simmering only one vegetable.

    True   False

9. A successful puree soup is made by simmering the main ingredient(s) until tender enough to mash easily.

    True   False

10. You can prepare a cream soup by simply adding cream or milk to a puree soup.

    True   False

UNIT 16 ANSWER KEY

A. Terminology

All definitions can be found in the text.

B. Short Answer

1. a. Broths: a clear liquid derived by simmering meaty cuts in water until a good flavor, body, and color develops.
   b. Consommés: clear soups made by combining a richly flavored stock or broth with a specific mixture of ingredients to produce a crystal clear soup with no traces of fat.
   c. Cream soups: made by simmering an ingredient in a thickened liquid, pureed for a very smooth texture, and finished with a quantity of cream, milk, or a liaison of egg yolks and cream.

2. a. Chowders: made with a base of broth, milk, or water, thickened by either a roux, and/or the inclusion of a starchy ingredient such as potatoes, rice, or beans.
   b. Gumbos: similar to chowders, are made with a brown roux, and often contain okra and/or gumbo file.
   c. Garbures: some or all of the ingredients are pureed, or starchy ingredients may be included so that the finished soup will have more body than a clear vegetable soup.

3. a. Combine the main ingredient with the liquid and bring to a slow simmer.
   b. Add remaining ingredients at appropriate intervals.
   c. Simmer until the broths flavor, color, and body develop.
   d. Make final adjustments to flavor, garnish, and serve the broth.
   e. Evaluate the quality of the finished broth.

4. a. Strainers: a fine wire mesh sieve, known as a bouillon strainer, a conical sieve lined with a coffee filter, or carefully rinsed cheesecloth
   b. A ladle to baste the raft as well as to dip the finished consommé out of the pot
   c. Tasting spoons
   d. Storage and service containers

C. Matching

   1. g
   2. f
   3. h
   4. j
   5. i

6. c
7. e
8. a
9. d
10. b

D. Multiple Choice

1. b
2. d
3. a
4. c
5. a
6. c
7. a
8. b
9. b
10. d

E. True or False

1. True
2. False
3. False
4. True
5. False
6. True
7. False
8. False
9. True
10. True

UNIT 17
SAUTÉING

A. Terminology: Fill in the blank space with the correct definition.

1. sauté _____

2. à la minute _____

3. sauté pans _____

4. sauteuse _____

5. cooking medium _____

6. sauce base _____

7. deglazing _____

8. finishing ingredients _____

9. garnishes _____

10. presentation side _____

11. fond _____

12. nappé _____

13. monté au beurre _____

B. Fill in the Blank: Fill in the blank with the word that best completes the sentence.

1. The great skill of the sauté chef is the ability to use this technique to maximize

every possible aspect of the food from its _____ to its

_____ to its _____.

2. In the sauté technique, the main item is usually kept _____

until you are ready to cook.

3. _____ _____ fish and those foods with

moderate amounts of fat (tuna and salmon, for instance) are typical choices

for sauté.

4. Both clarified butter and a variety of oils are popular for sautés since they can

reach _____ _____ without breaking

down.

5. The entire sauté technique takes place over relatively _____

heat.

6. Some foods have a better-looking side, known as the _____

side, the side facing up when you plate the dish.

C. Short Answer: Provide a short response that correctly answers each of the
questions below.

1. List the 7 steps of the sauté technique.

   a. _____

   b. _____

   c. _____

   d. _____

   e. _____

   f. _____

   g. _____

2. List 5 qualities of a good sauté pan.

   a. _____

   b. _____

c. _____

d. _____

e. _____

3. List the 5 steps for preparing foods for sautéing.

   a. _____

   b. _____

   c. _____

   d. _____

   e. _____

4. List the 5 main components of a sauce for a sauté.

   a. _____

   b. _____

   c. _____

   d. _____

   e. _____

5. List 4 ingredients that can be used to deglaze the sauté pan.

   a. _____

   b. _____

   c. _____

   d. _____

D. Multiple Choice: For each question, choose the one correct answer.

1. When you add foods to a hot pan:
   a. they raise the temperature of the pan
   b. they lower the temperature of the pan
   c. depending on the food item, they may or may not cause a change in the temperature of the pan
   d. they never cause a change in the temperature of the pan

2. The degree to which a food shrinks and loses moisture when you sauté it depends upon:
   a. proper selection
   b. advance preparation
   c. heat level while sautéing
   d. all of the above

3. During a sauté, the monté au beurre step is done:
   a. at the beginning of the sauté
   b. as the second step in the sauté
   c. just before the sauce is applied to the main item
   d. just after the sauce is applied to the main item

4. By definition, a sauté calls for:
   a. a small amount of fat
   b. a medium amount of fat
   c. a large amount of fat
   d. no fat at all

5. When considering the presentation of a sautéed dish, the focus should be on:
   a. the sauce
   b. the main item
   c. the plate
   d. the garnish

6. Searing is the:
   a. first stage of sautéing
   b. second stage of sautéing
   c. third stage of sautéing
   d. last stage of sautéing

7. Pinçage refers to:
   a. sweating
   b. smothering
   c. browning
   d. sautéing

8. The term fond refers to the drippings in the bottom of a sauté pan, and also can refer to:
   a. a stock
   b. a type of pan
   c. a liquor
   d. a finishing technique

E. True or False: Circle either True or False to indicate the correct answer.

1. Sautéing is considered an à la minute technique because it takes only a minute to complete.

   True   False

2. In sautéing, the chef has no control over the depth of color and degree of doneness in the finished product.

   True   False

3. The equipment for a sauté plays a significant role in how successful the sauté is.

   True   False

4. Sauté pans typically have sloped sides, a shape referred to as a sauteuse.

   True   False

5. A steam table or large pan with hot water kept on a back or side burner, known as a hot bain marie, keeps clarified butter, sauce bases, cream, and similar ingredients at 180degrees F or higher throughout service.

   True   False

6. The cooking fat used in sautéing simply lubricates the pan so that foods don't stick, and doesn't provide any other benefits to the technique.

   True   False

7. The first step for any sauté is to heat the pan and the cooking medium.

   True   False

8. When proteins are subjected to heat, they tighten up.

   True   False

9. You should have about two fluid ounces of sauce for each portion of sautéed food.

        True   False

10. Nappé is the term used to describe a sauce thick enough to cling to foods.

        True   False

UNIT 17 ANSWER KEY

A. Terminology

All definitions can be found in the text.

B. Fill in the Blank

1. flavor, color, texture
2. refrigerated
3. firm textured
4. high temperatures
5. high
6. presentation

C. Short Answer

1. a. Heat the pan and the cooking medium.
   b. Add the main item to the sauté pan properly.
   c. Turn the food item to finish cooking.
   d. Cook until properly done.
   e. Degrease and deglaze the pan.
   f. Add the sauce base, simmer, and finish.
   g. Serve the sautéed dish.

2. a. A very level, flat surface to conduct heat evenly
   b. Moderate to light gauge material that is light enough to heat quickly, but heavy enough to retain some heat
   c. Sloped sides to help release steam
   d. A long, securely attached handle
   e. The correct size to hold the food being sautéed (pans that are too big may scorch the food or the fond; pans that are too small may never develop a good color or reduced fond.)

3. a. Choose items that are naturally tender.
   b. Trim to remove fat, sinew, or connective tissue that might make them cook unevenly.
   c. Pound them to an even thickness, without crushing or pulverizing the food, if necessary.
   d. Dry the surface with absorbent paper toweling before applying seasonings.
   e. If desired, you may lightly dust foods to sauté with flour to keep them dry as they cook.

4. a. A liquid to deglaze the fond
   b. A sauce base
   c. Aromatics

126

        d. Finishing ingredients
        e. Garnishes

    5. a. Dry white or red wines
        b. Cognac or brandy
        c. Fruit or vegetable juices
        d. Water

D. Multiple Choice

    1. b
    2. d
    3. c
    4. a
    5. b
    6. a
    7. c
    8. a

E. True or False

    1. False
    2. False
    3. True
    4. True
    5. False
    6. False
    7. False
    8. True
    9. True
    10. True

UNIT 18
FRYING

A. Terminology: Fill in the blank space with the correct definition.

1. pan frying _____

2. deep frying _____

3. standard breading _____

4. frying oil or fat _____

5. recovery time _____

6. flavor transfer _____

7. swimming method _____

8. basket method _____

9. Panko bread crumbs _____

B. Fill in the Blank: Fill in the blank with the word that best completes the sentence.

1. The great skill of the sauté chef is the ability to use this technique to maximize every possible aspect of the food from its _____ to its _____ to its _____.

2. In the sauté technique, the main item is usually kept _____ until you are ready to cook.

3. _____ _____ fish and those with moderate amounts of fat (tuna and salmon, for instance) are typical choices for sauté.

4. Both clarified butter and a variety of oils are popular for sautés since they can reach _____ _____ without breaking down.

5. The entire sauté technique takes place over relatively _____ heat.

6. Some foods have a better-looking side, known as the _____ side, the side facing up when you plate the dish.

7. In pan-frying, food is cooked by the oil's _____ rather than by _____ _____ with the pan.

8. Pan-fried foods are best when they are served _____ _____, straight from the _____.

9. Most pan-fried dishes include a _____ _____, a _____, _____, and a cooking medium.

10. Foods for pan-frying are naturally _____ and of a size and shape that can _____ _____.

11. _____ is the most common cooking medium when you pan fry.

12. Pan-frying does not generate a fond, so, in general, any sauce you choose is made _____.

13. When pan-frying, if you are using a simple coating of flour or a batter, add

them to the food _____ _____ it goes

into the fat.

14. Getting pan-fried foods evenly browned and crisped requires that the food be

in _____ _____ with the hot fat.

C. Short Answer: Provide a short response that correctly answers each of the
    questions below.

1. List 4 guidelines for choosing oil or fat for use in pan-frying.

    a. _____

    b. _____

    c. _____

    d. _____

2. List 4 guidelines for step one in pan-frying—heating the fat.

    a. _____

    b. _____

    c. _____

    d. _____

3. List 6 steps to maintain the quality of the oil in your deep fryer.

    a. _____

    b. _____

    c. _____

d. _____

e. _____

f. _____

4. When applying the Frying Technique:

List 2 main ingredient options:

a. _____

b. _____

List 2 flavoring and seasoning options:

a. _____

b. _____

List 2 coating options:

a. _____

b. _____

D. Multiple Choice: For each question, choose the one correct answer.

1. Fried foods are best served:
   a. cold
   b. warm
   c. at room temperature
   d. very hot

2. Pan-fried food is fried in enough oil to cover it by:
   a. one-quarter
   b. one-third
   c. half to two-thirds
   d. completely

3. The basic characteristics of a good pan for frying are:
   a. heavy gauge and able to transmit heat evenly (for example, cast iron pans)
   b. large enough to hold foods in a single layer
   c. straight sides, high enough to keep oil from splashing out of the pan
   d. all of the above

4. A fat with a high smoking point:
   a. does not stand up to extended use
   b. does stand up to extended use
   c. can only be used once
   d. can be used indefinitely

5. Standard breading is prepared by coating foods with:
   a. only flour
   b. only flour and egg wash
   c. only egg wash and breadcrumbs
   d. flour, egg wash, and breadcrumbs

6. When making an egg wash, a general guideline calls for:
   a. about 1 ounce of milk for every 2 whole eggs
   b. about 1 ounce of milk for every 3 whole eggs
   c. about 2 ounces of milk for every 2 whole eggs
   d. about 4 ounces of milk for every 2 whole eggs

7. When you have finished performing the standard breading procedure, the flour, egg wash, and breadcrumbs should be:
   a. discarded
   b. refrigerated
   c. sifted and/or strained
   d. covered and stored at room temperature

8. Deep-frying calls for:
   a. foods that take a considerable time to cook
   b. tender foods
   c. foods that are tough
   d. foods that cannot be pan-fried

E. True or False: Circle either True or False to indicate the correct answer.

1. Weiner schnitzel is a traditional dish from France.

               True   False

2. Deep-fried foods are cooked in enough fat or oil to completely submerge them.

               True   False

3. Electric or gas deep fryers with baskets are typically used for pan-frying.

               True   False

4. The same foods that can be pan-fried can also be deep-fried.

    True   False

5. Fats and oils do not differ in flavor or composition.

    True   False

6. When frying moist items, dry them as thoroughly as possible before placing them in oil, because water breaks down the oil and lowers the smoking point.

    True   False

7. The coating for a deep-fried food serves the same function as it does for a pan-fried food.

    True   False

8. Selecting and using the right cooking oils is important whether you are pan-frying or deep-frying.

    True   False

UNIT 18 ANSWER SHEET

A. Terminology

All definitions can be found in the text.

B. Fill in the Blank

1. heat, direct contact
2. very hot, pan
3. main ingredient, coating, seasonings
4. tender, cook quickly
5. Oil
6. separately
7. just before
8. direct contact

C. Short Answer

1. a. Use fresh oil or fat for the best results.
   b. Choose an oil or fat able to reach and maintain frying temperatures without excessive foaming or smoking.
   c. Vegetable oils such as corn, canola, and safflower have neutral flavors.
   d. Olive oil, lard, goose fat, and other rendered animal fats add their own flavor to a dish and have a place in certain regional and ethnic dishes.

2. a. Add enough fat to come half to two-thirds of the way up the food.
   b. The thinner the food, the less fat is required.
   c. When a faint haze or slight shimmer is noticeable, the fat is hot enough.
   d. Test the temperature of the fat or oil: Dip a corner of the food in the fat. When the fat is at about 350degrees F/175 degrees C, it bubbles around the food and the coating starts to brown within 45 seconds.

3. a. Use high-quality oil.
   b. Prevent the oil from coming in contact with copper, brass, or bronze, because these metals hasten breakdown.
   c. When frying moist items, dry them as thoroughly as possible before placing them in oil.
   d. Do not salt products over the deep-fryer because salt breaks down the oil.
   e. Fry items at the proper temperature. Do not overheat the oil.
   f. Keep the fryer and baskets clean. Constantly remove any small particles from the oil during use.

4. Main ingredient options:

   a. Remove the skin and bones of poultry and fish fillets if necessary or desired.
   b. Cooked foods can be bound with a heavy béchamel and shaped into croquettes before they are breaded and fried.

   Flavoring and seasoning options:

   a. Stuffings, marinades, or other ingredients are often used in pan-fried dishes.
   b. Additional ingredients may be added to the standard breading ingredients (i.e., ground nuts or grated Parmesan cheese in the breadcrumbs).

   Coating options:

   a. Add finely chopped nuts or grated cheese to the breading in a standard breading.
   b. Use a batter instead of standard breading.

D. Multiple Choice

   1. d
   2. c
   3. d
   4. b
   5. d
   6. d
   7. a
   8. b

E. True or False

   1. False
   2. True
   3. False
   4. True
   5. False
   6. True
   7. True
   8. True

A. Terminology: Fill in the blank space with the correct definition.

1. bake _____

2. bard _____

3. baste _____

4. carry-over cooking _____

5. deglaze _____

6. jus _____

7. jus lié _____

8. lard _____

9. pan gravy _____

10. poêlé _____

11. roast _____

12. smoke-roasting _____

13. truss _____

B. Short Answer: Provide a short response that correctly answers each of the questions below.

1. List 3 things that are important in selecting the proper roasting pan.

a. _____

b. _____

c. _____

2. List 6 items you will need during roasting as well as for service.

   a. _____

   b. _____

   c. _____

   d. _____

   e. _____

   f. _____

3. List 4 seasoning options for preparing foods to be roasted.

   a. _____

   b. _____

   c. _____

   d. _____

C. Multiple Choice: For each question, choose the one correct answer.

   1. The amount of time a roast should rest depends on:
      a. the oven temperature
      b. the room temperature
      c. how big the roast is
      d. how long the roast has been in the oven

   2. Roasted items that are too pale not only lack visual appeal but also:
      a. tenderness
      b. a correct degree of doneness
      c. a safe degree of doneness
      d. depth of flavor

   3. An optional first step in roasting is:
      a. searing
      b. braising
      c. steaming
      d. poaching

4. Both smoke roasting and poêléing are exceptions to the general statement that you should:
   a. roast foods at low temperatures
   b. roast foods uncovered
   c. roast foods that are tender
   d. roast foods that are tough

5. Foods placed on a rod that is turned either manually or with a motor and cooked by radiant heat are cooked by what method?
   a. smoke-roasted
   b. slow-baked
   c. spit-roasted
   d. butter-roasted

6. Pan gravy is made by thickening a rich broth or stock with:
   a. a roux
   b. a slurry
   c. a reduction
   d. a fond

7. The last step in making a jus or a jus lié is:
   a. bringing it to a boil
   b. draining the mirepoix through a strainer
   c. deglazing with an appropriate liquid
   d. straining and adjusting the seasoning

8. Roasting is one of the:
   a. oldest cooking techniques
   b. newest cooking techniques
   c. simplest cooking techniques
   d. hardest cooking techniques

D. True or False: Circle either True or False to indicate the correct answer.

1. Basting foods as they cook further improves their flavor and texture.

   True   False

2. Deciding which foods to call roasted and which to call baked is largely a matter of preference.

   True   False

3. The more marbling in the meat, the less tender and moist it will be after it is roasted.

   True   False

138

4. The skin is normally removed from birds when they are roasted.

        True   False

5. An initial searing can only be performed either over direct heat.

        True   False

6. Leaving roasts uncovered as they cook helps them develop a good texture.

        True   False

7. It is important not to take foods out of the oven before they reach the temperature you'd like them to have for service.

        True   False

8. Resting allows the juices in the roast to redistribute themselves for a good texture and flavor in the carved roast.

        True   False

UNIT 19 ANSWER KEY

A. Terminology

All definitions can be found in the text.

B. Short Answer

1. a. A heavy, flat bottom
   b. Low sides
   c. Correct size to hold the food comfortably

2. a. Basting brush to apply basting sauce
   b. Instant-read thermometer to check doneness
   c. Butcher's twine or skewers for trussing or tying
   d. Holding pan to hold roast while preparing sauce
   e. Carving tools, including a slicer, honing steel, and fork
   f. Saucepan, strainers, and skimmers to prepare sauce

3. a. Salt
   b. Freshly ground black pepper
   c. Brining or marinating
   d. Dry or wet herb or spice rubs

C. Multiple Choice

1. c
2. d
3. a
4. b
5. c
6. a
7. d
8. a

D. True or False

1. True
2. True
3. False
4. False
5. False
6. True
7. False
8. True

A. Terminology: Fill in the blank space with the correct definition.

1. barbecue _____

2. dry rub _____

3. marinade _____

4. brine _____

5. sop, mop, and basting sauce _____

6. barbecue sauce _____

7. smoke _____

B. Fill in the Blank: Fill in the blank with the word that best completes the sentence.

1. Barbeques are sometimes referred to as _____.

2. Basting sauces are also known as _____ or

   _____.

3. In the eastern part of the Carolinas, barbeque sauce is traditionally based upon

   _____.

4. In south Texas, _____ is also popular for barbeque.

5. In the Northwestern part of the United States, _____ is

   often "barbecued" along with other types of fish and seafood.

6. The thick, tomato-y style of _____

   _____ barbecue sauce has become the prototype for

   commercial sauces sold nationwide.

7. Most would agree that barbecuing is the _____,

_____, _____ cooking of meat at low

temperatures with smoke in order to produce tender and extremely flavorful

meats.

8. Throughout the south, with the exception of Texas, you are more likely to find

_____ than _____ used for barbeque.

C. Short Answer: Provide a short response that correctly answers each of the questions below.

1. List 3 facts that most practitioners and fans of barbeque agree on.

    a. _____

    b. _____

    c. _____

2. List 5 pieces of equipment needed to complete the barbeque process.

    a. _____

    b. _____

    c. _____

    d. _____

    e. _____

3. List 3 types of social settings where barbeque is used as the focal point.

    a. _____

    b. _____

    c. _____

D. Multiple Choice: For each question, choose the one correct answer.

1. Traditional side dishes at barbeques are:
    a. cole slaw
    b. corn bread
    c. boiled potatoes
    d. all of the above

2. A smoke ring is:
    a. a bluish ring found within smoked meats
    b. a black ring found within smoked meats
    c. a reddish ring found within smoked meats
    d. a piece of equipment found on a smoker

3. Dry rubs are applied to meats in a layer and:
    a. wiped off after 10 minutes
    b. wiped off after 1 hour
    c. washed off just before barbequing
    d. left on the meat for several hours, or days, before the meat is barbequed

4. A white barbeque sauce has as its base:
    a. mayonnaise
    b. heavy cream
    c. béchamel sauce
    d. plain yogurt

5. Jerk is a barbeque technique found in:
    a. the Carolinas
    b. Kansas City
    c. Memphis
    d. the Caribbean

6. If _____ is added to a Memphis-Style barbeque sauce it becomes an amalgam of all the major components of barbeque sauce.
    a. brown sugar
    b. mustard
    c. molasses
    d. ketchup

7. The exact origin of the word barbeque is:
    a. unclear
    b. definitely from the Arawak language
    c. Christopher Columbus
    d. European

E. True or False: Circle either True or False to indicate the correct answer.

1. Barbequed foods are generally cooked at high temperatures for long periods of time.

    True   False

2. Pork is the only real barbeque.

    True   False

3. The traditions and history of barbecue show that this technique evolved as a way to make tough, well-exercised meats very tender.

    True   False

4. Direct heat cooks meat at 300 to 350degrees F, and is often used for smaller and more tender cuts that cook more quickly (seafood or poultry, for instance).

    True   False

5. A dry rub is never left on the meat for more than one day before the meat is cooked.

    True   False

6. Marinades typically contain an oil, but no acid.

    True   False

7. Basting sauces are applied to barbecued foods as they cook.

    True   False

8. There are 6 distinct styles of barbeque in the United States.

    True   False

9. Ribs, however, remain the most well known meat in Memphis barbecue.

    True   False

10. The thick, tomato-y style of Kansas City barbecue sauce has become the prototype for commercial sauces sold nationwide.

    True   False

144

UNIT 20 ANSWER SHEET

A. Terminology

All definitions can be found in the text.

B. Fill in the Blank

1. pits
2. mops, sops
3. vinegar
4. cabrito
5. salmon
6. Kansas City
7. long, slow, gentle
8. pork, beef

C. Short Answer

1. a. Barbecue is not the same as grilling, even if you grill foods with a barbecue sauce.
   b. Barbecuing requires smoke to properly flavor and color the food.
   c. Barbecued foods are cooked at low temperatures for long periods in order to develop the best flavor and an extremely tender texture.

2. a. Containers to hold meats as they brine or marinate
   b. Brushes or mops to apply basting and finishing sauces
   c. Cutting boards
   d. Pots to keep basting and barbeque sauces at a simmer
   e. Knives to slice or chop meats, or gloves if you are to pull meats apart

3. a. Church suppers
   b. Political gatherings
   c. Community or neighborhood gatherings

D. Multiple Choice

1. d
2. c
3. d
4. a
5. d
6. b
7. a

E. True or False

1. False
2. False
3. True
4. True
5. False
6. False
7. False
8. False
9. True
10. True

A. Terminology: Fill in the blank space with the correct definition.

1. radiant heat _____

2. broiling _____

3. grilling _____

4. zones _____

5. à l'anglaise _____

6. compound butter _____

7. radiant heat _____

8. skewers _____

9. basting sauce _____

10. glazing sauce _____

11. gratinéed _____

12. crosshatch marks _____

B. Short Answer: Provide a short response that correctly answers each of the questions below.

1. List 4 steps for preparing a grill.

    a. _____

    b. _____

    c. _____

    d. _____

2. List 5 major factors in successfully grilling or broiling.

   a. _____

   b. _____

   c. _____

   d. _____

   e. _____

3. List 5 food items commonly griddled.

   a. _____

   b. _____

   c. _____

   d. _____

   e. _____

C. Matching: Match each of the terms in List A with the appropriate description in List B.

List A	*List B*
___ 1. grilling	a. the best looking side of the food
___ 2. the grill station	b. used to add moisture to very lean cuts
___ 3. grill brush	c. dry-heat cooking method
___ 4. hand racks	d. their connective tissues and proteins cook at lower temperatures
___ 5. caul fat	e. used to scour the grill rods
___ 6. coulis and salsa	f. one of the most demanding line positions
___ 7. presentation side	g. saucing options for grilled foods
___ 8. fish and shellfish	h. used when grilling delicate foods

D. Multiple Choice: For each question, choose the one correct answer.

1. Grilling and broiling are most often used for:
   a. large roasts
   b. whole fish
   c. portion sized cuts
   d. all of the above

2. In order to achieve the characteristic crosshatch marks you need:
   a. a well heated grill
   b. a moist surface on the meat
   c. a long cooking time
   d. a gas fired grill

3. A hot bed of coals:
   a. has a slight ash coating
   b. glows red
   c. has a thick ash coating
   d. has a slight red glow

4. Identifying hot and cool zones on the grill allows you to:
   a. grill tougher cuts of meat
   b. avoid sticking or charring
   c. flavor the items more successfully
   d. control cooking speed

5. For successful grilling always choose cuts that are
   a. of a relatively even thickness
   b. thin enough to cook properly
   c. trimmed appropriately
   d. all of the above

6. If you are using wooden skewers for grilling you should:
   a. use skewers no longer than 5 inches
   b. use skewers that have been soaked in water
   c. use skewers that are sharpened on both ends
   d. use skewers made of hardened plastic

E. True or False: Circle either True or False to indicate the correct answer.

1. The traditional wisdom that fish is properly cooked when it flakes easily is true.

    True   False

2. The surface of a properly grilled food should appear moist, with the characteristic deep-brown cross-hatch marks.

       True   False

3. Broiled foods should have a light-brown color.

       True   False

4. If grilled food has a rubbery or tough texture, it was undercooked or allowed to cook too slowly.

       True   False

5. A compound butter is a simple but appropriate sauce for grilled foods.

       True   False

6. Most foods that can be grilled cannot be broiled.

       True   False

7. Various coatings can be used to top broiled food, offering a layer of protection to keep foods moist, and add flavor and texture contrast at the same time.

       True   False

8. Glazed means that foods are coated with cheese and breadcrumbs, known as a glaçage.

       True   False

9. Royal glaçage is made by combining equal parts Hollandaise sauce, velouté, and whipped heavy cream.

       True   False

UNIT 21 ANSWER KEY

A. Terminology

All definitions can be found in the text.

B. Short Answer

1. a. Thoroughly clean and properly heat the grill to prevent foods from sticking or charring.
   b. Divide the grill or broiler into zones both to prevent flavor transfer and to keep track of the items' doneness during a busy service period.
   c. Identify hot and cool zones on the grill in order to control cooking speed.
   d. Keep a grill brush on hand to scour the rods as you cook and a cloth to lightly rub the rods with oil.

2. a. Selecting the proper cuts of meat, poultry, and seafood
   b. Knowing how to determine the appropriate doneness
   c. Choosing or preparing cuts of a relatively even thickness
   d. Choosing or preparing cuts that are thin enough to cook properly without excessive exterior charring
   e. Trimming away fat, silverskin, and gristle

3. a. Pancakes
   b. Eggs
   c. Potatoes
   d. Sausages
   e. Sandwiches

C. Matching

   1. c
   2. f
   3. e
   4. h
   5. b
   6. g
   7. a
   8. d

D. Multiple Choice

   1. c
   2. a

3. b
4. d
5. d
6. b

E. True or False

1. False
2. True
3. False
4. False
5. True
6. False
7. True
8. False
9. True

UNIT 22
BRAISING AND STEWING

A. Terminology: Fill in the blank space with the correct definition.

1. braise _____

2. stew _____

3. sear _____

4. sieze _____

5. reduce _____

6. glaze _____

7. fork tender _____

B. Fill in the Blank: Fill in the blank with the word that best completes the sentence.

1. Braising and stewing are known as _____ cooking

   methods.

2. A good braise or stew has a _____

   _____ and intensely flavored, complex

   _____.

3. Braises are cooked in enough liquid to cover them by

   _____ to _____ their depth.

4. Stews are made by cutting the food into bite-sized pieces and then cooking

   them in enough liquid to _____ _____

   them.

5. In braises and stews the sauce gets its flavor from the combination of the

   _____ _____, the

   _____, and the flavor of the _____ itself.

6. Braising and stewing are traditionally paired with cuts of meat from more

   _____ _____ of the animal.

7. Stewing, similar to braising, can use the same meat cuts, but the main item is

   cut into _____ pieces, typically a _____

   _____.

8. A Mediterranean-style fish stew combining a variety of fish and shellfish is

   called a _____.

9. _____ is a French term for stew, which literally translates

   as "restores the appetite."

10. A _____ is a white stew traditionally made from white

    meats (veal or chicken) or lamb, and is garnished with mushrooms and pearl

    onions.

C. Matching: Match each of the terms in List A with the appropriate description in
   List B.

List A	*List B*
___1. braising and stewing	a. French term for a braising method and the braised dish itself
___2. braises	b. initial browning step which takes place over direct heat
___3. stews	c. a white stew

_____4. aromatics

d. a stew that originated in Hungary and is seasoned and colored with paprika

_____5. searing

e. combination cooking methods

_____6. estouffade

f. mirepoix, tomato paste, bouquet garni

_____7. fricassée

g. made from larger pieces of food

_____8. goulash

h. made with bite-sized pieces of food

D. Multiple Choice: For each question, choose the one correct answer.

1. Braises and stews are usually made from:
    a. tougher cuts of meat
    b. whole birds
    c. firm fleshed fish or shellfish
    d. all of the above

2. When searing the food item to be braised the oil should be:
    a. smoking hot
    b. very hot
    c. not very hot
    d. moderately hot

3. Mirepoix is added to a braise to:
    a. introduce moisture
    b. introduce flavor
    c. introduce moisture and flavor
    d. introduce a tenderizing effect

4. Flour or roux should be added to a braise:
    a. as a first step
    b. after the mirepoix is cooked
    c. after deglazing the pan
    d. at the end of the cooking process

5. If possible, the liquid used to braise foods should be:
    a. brought to a simmer separately over direct heat and then added
    b. added cold and slowly brought to a simmer
    c. added cold and quickly brought to a simmer
    d. added when it is already boiling

6. During the braising process additional liquid should:
    a. never be added
    b. added only at the beginning
    c. added only at the end
    d. added if necessary

7. Braised foods are cooked until:
   a. they fall into shreds
   b. they can just barely be pierced with a fork
   c. they are tender enough to slide off a kitchen fork easily
   d. they give a slight resistance to being pierced with a pairing knife

8. A daube is a braise customarily made from:
   a. red meats
   b. chicken
   c. fish
   d. game birds

E. True or False: Circle either True or False to indicate the correct answer.

1. Perfectly braised or stewed foods have a somewhat bland flavor and only a mildly soft texture.

    True   False

2. In braising and stewing, foods undergo only one phase of cooking.

    True   False

3. In braising, the mirepoix should always be cut into large dice.

    True   False

4. Braised foods should have an intense flavor as the result of long, gentle cooking.

    True   False

5. Braised foods lose very little amount of volume during cooking.

    True   False

6. In the benchmark recipe Braised Lamb Shanks, a sauce, jus de veau lié, is combined with wine for a braising liquid that is aromatic and flavorful enough to stand up to the intense flavor of the lamb.

    True   False

7. Pot roast, a common American term for braising, is also the name of a traditional braised dish.

       True   False

8. A stew's components do not differ to any substantial degree from those of a braise.

       True   False

A. Terminology

All definitions can be found in the text.

B. Fill in the Blank

1. combination
2. soft texture, sauce
3. one-third, one-half
4. completely submerge
5. main ingredient, aromatics, liquid
6. exercised portions
7. bite-sized, 1- to 2-inch cube
8. Bouillabaisse
9. Ragout
10. Blanquette

C. Matching

1. e
2. g
3. h
4. f
5. b
6. a
7. c
8. d

D. Multiple Choice

1. d
2. b
3. c
4. b
5. a
6. d
7. c
8. a

E. True or False

    1. False
    2. False
    3. False
    4. True
    5. False
    6. True
    7. True
    8. True

UNIT 23
SHALLOW-POACHING

A. Terminology: Fill in the blank space with the correct definition.

1. shallow poach _____

2. paupiettes _____

3. en papillote _____

4. poaching liquid (cuisson) _____

5. vin blanc sauce _____

6. reduction _____

B. Short Answer: Provide a short response that correctly answers each of the questions below.

1. List 5 guidelines for a shallow-poaching pan.

   a. _____

   b. _____

   c. _____

   d. _____

   e. _____

2. List 3 types of food suitable for shallow poaching.

   a. _____

   b. _____

   c. _____

3. List 3 options when it comes to saucing a shallow-poached dish.

   a. _____

   b. _____

   c. _____

C. Multiple Choice: For each question, choose the one correct answer.

   1. In shallow poaching, the poaching liquid is called:
      a. cuisson
      b. vin blanc
      c. fond
      d. paupiette

   2. A paupiette is most often made from:
      a. boneless chicken breasts
      b. fish fillets
      c. mousseline forcemeat
      d. fish steaks

   3. Scattering aromatics or vegetables over the bottom of the pan:
      a. keeps the food from sticking
      b. provides the moisture for shallow poaching
      c. acts as a "rack"
      d. is seldom done in shallow poaching

   4. The amount of liquid used in shallow poaching is determined by:
      a. the length of the cooking time
      b. the type of food you are cooking
      c. the quantity of food you are cooking
      d. all of the above

   5. The temperature of the poaching liquid should not rise above:
      a. 150 degrees F
      b. 160 degrees F
      c. 170 degrees F
      d. 180 degrees F

   6. When well-prepared, shallow-poached dishes reflect the flavor of:
      a. the food being poached
      b. the cooking liquid
      c. the flavoring and aromatics added to the liquid
      d. all of the above

161

7. En papillote translates literally as:
   a. "in paper"
   b. "in foil"
   c. "in leaves"
   d. "in wrappers"

8. Steaming has wide application in the preparation of:
   a. vegetables
   b. couscous
   c. Chinese-style dumplings
   d. all of the above

D. True or False: Circle either True or False to indicate the correct answer.

1. In shallow poaching, the amount of liquid is determined by the type and quantity of food you are cooking as well as the dish's cooking time.

       True   False

2. It is preferable to prepare shallow-poached foods over direct heat from start to finish.

       True   False

3. Shallow-poached foods are cooked until they are just done.

       True   False

4. To make a sauce vin blanc, simply reduce the poaching liquid (cuisson) and add the desired aromatics.

       True   False

5. In steaming, foods cook in a closed environment by the steam or vapor that surrounds them.

       True   False

6. Steaming is not generally used in the preparation of vegetables.

       True   False

7. The disadvantages of steaming include the loss of water-soluble vitamins.

       True   False

8. The classic wrapper for a dish en papillote is aluminum foil.

     True   False

9. Shallow poaching, cooking foods en papillote, and steaming are gentle cooking techniques best suited to tender, almost delicate foods, especially fish, seafood, and poultry.

     True   False

10. Shallow poaching is often done in a sautoir or similar pan; a "lid" of buttered parchment helps trap the steam for even and rapid cooking.

     True   False

UNIT 23 ANSWER KEY

A. Terminology

All definitions can be found in the text.

B. Short Answer

1. a. Select a pan that is just large enough to hold the food and the cooking liquid comfortably.
   b. Shallow and wide enough to ensure even, rapid cooking as well as to make transferring the ingredients into or out of the pan easy
   c. Wide enough to encourage rapid reduction of cooking liquid as you prepare the sauce
   d. Medium or moderate gauge pans for heat retention as well as some level of responsiveness to changes to cooking speed
   e. Choose pans made from non-reactive materials (stainless steel, anodized aluminum) to avoid discoloring sauce.

2. a. Boneless skinless poultry breast portions
   b. Fish fillets or steaks cut into portions
   c. Mussels, clams, or oysters (in the shell or shocked)

3. a. Diced chilled butter to finish the sauce
   b. A prepared sauce base, such as a velouté, reduced heavy cream, or purées
   c. Additional finishing and garnishing ingredients such as fresh herbs, and citrus zest

C. Multiple Choice

   1. a
   2. b
   3. c
   4. d
   5. d
   6. d
   7. a
   8. d

D. True or False

   1. True
   2. False
   3. True
   4. False

5. True
6. False
7. False
8. False
9. True
10. True

UNIT 24
POACHING AND SIMMERING

A. Terminology: Fill in the blank space with the correct definition.

1. simmer _____

2. poach _____

3. cooking liquid/poaching liquid _____

   _____

4. court bouillon _____

B. Fill in the Blank: Fill in the blank with the word that best completes the sentence.

1. Poaching and simmering are _____

   _____ cooking techniques.

2. Boiling is most appropriate for dry, dense, starchy foods that need to be

   _____.

3. The aim of poaching is to produce foods that are _____ and

   extremely _____.

4. To bring the poaching liquid up to temperature more quickly, use a

   _____-_____ _____.

5. Simmering is best suited for meats with a more pronounced

   _____.

6. Some foods that are referred to as boiled are actually

   _____.

7. If desired, tie stuffed meats to maintain their _____.

8. If necessary, the surface of the poaching liquid should be

   _____.

9. Let the poaching liquid drain away from the food by setting it on a

   _____.

10. Deep-poached poultry and meats are cooked until _____

    _____.

C. Short Answer: Provide a short response that correctly answers each of the questions below.

   1. List 3 guidelines for pots to be used for deep poaching.

      a. _____

      b. _____

      c. _____

   2. List 5 foods suitable for poaching.

      a. _____

      b. _____

      c. _____

      d. _____

      e. _____

   3. List 5 foods suitable for simmering.

      a. _____

      b. _____

c. _____

d. _____

e. _____

D. Multiple Choice: For each question, choose the one correct answer.

1. For poaching fish or shellfish, the liquid can be:
   a. fish stock
   b. wine
   c. court bouillon
   d. all of the above

2. When the poaching liquid is "shivering":
   a. the surface of the liquid shows no motion
   b. the surface of the liquid may show some motion
   c. the surface of the liquid shows air bubbles
   d. the surface of the liquid shows rapid motion

3. If part of the food is above the level of the cooking liquid, the cooking will be:
   a. uneven
   b. quicker
   c. slower
   d. result in better color

4. The most accurate test for doneness is to check:
   a. the poaching liquid's temperature
   b. the firmness of the food item
   c. the food's internal temperature
   d. the color of the food item

5. Remove poached salmon from the liquid when it reaches a temperature of:
   a. 125 degrees F
   b. 145 degrees F
   c. 165 degrees F
   d. 175 degrees F

6. When checking for doneness, any juices from poultry are:
   a. a light pink color
   b. a medium red color
   c. a dark red color
   d. nearly colorless

7. When checking for doneness, the flesh of fish and shellfish is:
   a. translucent
   b. very firm
   c. nearly opaque
   d. rubbery

8. If a poached or simmered item is to be served cold, you should:
   a. slightly undercook it
   b. pull the pot from the heat and leave it uncovered
   c. add ice to the liquid to stop the cooking
   d. remove the food from the liquid before it is fully cooked

E. True or False: Circle either True or False to indicate the correct answer.

   1. There are no similarities in the techniques of poaching and simmering.

      True   False

   2. Poaching calls for a higher temperature than does simmering.

      True   False

   3. The pot used for deep poaching should hold the food, liquid, and aromatics comfortably, with enough room to allow the liquid to expand as it heats.

      True   False

   4. Items to be deep poached should be naturally tender.

      True   False

   5. Poached foods are never served with a sauce that includes some of the poaching liquid.

      True   False

   6. Once poaching has begun, additional liquid should not be added because it will throw off the cooking time.

      True   False

   7. The most accurate test for doneness when poaching or simmering is firmness to the touch.

      True   False

8. Properly poached salmon should flake easily.

    True   False

9. Equipment needs for simmering are the same as those for poaching.

    True   False

10. Items to be simmered are often more mature and less tender than cuts you might choose for poaching.

    True   False

UNIT 24 ANSWER KEY

A. Terminology

All definitions can be found in the text.

B. Fill in the Blank

1. moist heat
2. rehydrated
3. moist, tender
4. tight-fitting lid
5. texture
6. simmered
7. shape
8. skimmed
9. rack
10. just tender

C. Short Answer

1. a. Wide enough space to allow you to skim the surface as necessary
      throughout the cooking process
   b. A rack or insert that lets you lower the food into the liquid and lift it out
      easily, without breaking it apart, as well as to keep the food lifted up from
      the bottom of the pan during poaching
   c. A tight-fitting lid helps to bring the liquid up to temperature more quickly,
      but it is not used during actual deep poaching. (Leaving a lid on
      throughout the cooking process may actually cause the liquid to become
      hotter than desired.)

2. a. Sole
   b. Flounder
   c. Halibut
   d. Salmon
   e. Sweetbreads

3. a. Corned beef
   b. Tongue
   c. Brisket
   d. Lobster
   e. Shrimp

D. Multiple Choice

1. d
2. b
3. a
4. c
5. b
6. d
7. c
8. a

E. True or False

1. False
2. False
3. True
4. True
5. False
6. False
7. False
8. False
9. True
10. True

UNIT 25
VEGETABLES

A. Terminology: Fill in the blank space with the correct definition.

1. blanch _____

2. parcook _____

3. refresh _____

4. steaming _____

5. pan-steaming and oven-steaming _____

6. gratins _____

B. Fill in the Blank: Fill in the blank with the word that best completes the sentence.

1. Pan-steamed vegetables are prepared in a _____.

2. Steam roasting is suitable for dense winter vegetables such as

   _____ or _____.

3. Grilled vegetables have a distinctive _____ flavor.

4. Pierce vegetables that you will be roasting, otherwise they may

   _____.

5. When sautéing vegetables, choose a cooking fat that _____

   the flavor of the vegetables.

6. In Pan-frying, the amount of oil used as a cooking medium is

   _____ than for sautéing.

7. In deep frying, once the correct temperature is reached, adjust the heat so that the temperature remains relatively _____.

8. Stewed or braised vegetables literally cook in their own

    _____.

9. The vegetables in a stew are customarily cut into _____ pieces.

10. When reheating vegetables by sautéing, toss over _____ heat.

C. Multiple Choice: For each question, choose the one correct answer.

1. Most vegetables are best when:
   a. simmered
   b. boiled
   c. roasted
   d. sautéed

2. When vegetables are cooked to the proper doneness, they should be:
   a. fully cooked and tender
   b. fully cooked and very soft
   c. fully cooked and falling apart
   d. partially cooked and very firm

3. To preserve the best flavor, texture, and nutritional value in cooked vegetables, serve them:
   a. a reasonable length of time after cooking
   b. as soon as possible after cooking
   c. no more than 1 hour after cooking
   d. no more than 2 hours after cooking

4. In blanching, vegetables are immersed briefly, usually:
   a. 5 to 30 seconds
   b. 30 seconds to 1 minute
   c. 1 to 3 minutes
   d. 3 to 5 minutes

5. Al dente is an Italian term used to describe the desired doneness of:
   a. poultry
   b. meat
   c. vegetables
   d. pasta

6. Steaming shares many similarities with _____ as a cooking technique for vegetables.
   a. sautéing
   b. grilling
   c. roasting
   d. boiling

7. Adding chopped, toasted walnuts to pan-steamed green beans adds:
   a. contrasting texture
   b. additional flavor
   c. another level of interest to the dish
   d. all of the above

8. Pan frying is similar to:
   a. grilling
   b. roasting
   c. broiling
   d. sautéing

9. The best temperature for deep frying most vegetables is about:
   a. 300 degrees F
   b. 325 degrees F
   c. 350 degrees F
   d. 375 degrees F

10. Vegetables for a braise may be _____ to set their colors.
    a. simmered
    b. blanched
    c. steamed
    d. roasted

D. True or False: Circle either True or False to indicate the correct answer.

1. The only way to reheat vegetables is by simmering in stock or water.

   True   False

2. Steamed and boiled vegetables are only served hot.

   True   False

3. Most vegetables are best when cooked at a hard boil.

> True   False

4. Boiled vegetables are cooked in a large amount of water.

> True   False

5. The only way to determine how tender a vegetable should be when it is properly cooked is by how you intend to serve or use it.

> True   False

6. Parboiled vegetables are cooked to partial doneness, to prepare them to be finished by grilling, sautéing, or stewing.

> True   False

7. Vegetables you will finish by sautéing in butter or adding to stews or braises need not be fully cooked in all cases (blanched or parcooked is best).

> True   False

8. In the steaming method, a hard boil is not necessary.

> True   False

UNIT 25 ANSWER KEY

A. Terminology

All definitions can be found in the text.

B. Fill in the Blank

1. covered pot
2. winter squash, beets
3. charred
4. explode
5. compliments
6. greater
7. constant
8. juices
9. small
10. medium-high

C. Multiple Choice

1. a
2. a
3. b
4. b
5. d
6. d
7. d
8. d
9. c
10. b

D. True or False

1. False
2. False
3. False
4. True
5. False
6. True
7. True
8. True

UNIT 26
STARCHES

A. Terminology: Fill in the blank space with the correct definition.

1. starches _____

2. pasta _____

3. noodles _____

4. grains _____

5. legumes _____

6. pilaf _____

7. risotto _____

8. puree _____

B. Short Answer: Provide a short response that correctly answers each of the questions below.

1. List the 3 basic types of starches, and give three examples of each one.

a. _____

_____

b. _____

_____

c. _____

_____

2. List 4 qualities of a properly boiled potato.

a. _____

b. _____

c. _____

d. _____

3. List 3 additional ingredients that can be added to puréed potatoes for richness, color, and flavor, and at what temperature they should be when they are added.

   a. _____

   _____

   b. _____

   _____

   c. _____

   _____

4. List 3 procedures for preparing whole potatoes for roasting.

   a. _____

   b. _____

   c. _____

C. Matching: Match each of the terms in List A with the appropriate description in List B.

List A	*List B*
___1. starches	a. jackets
___2. waxy yellow potatoes	b. tender, but with a distinct bite
___3. potato skins	c. an Italian rice dish
___4. parching	d. puréed potatoes made with egg yolks
___5. risotto	e. Yellow Finn and Yukon Gold
___6. mantecuro	f. a significant source of nutrition worldwide

____7. al dente

g. heating the grain in hot fat or oil

____8. Duchesse potatoes

h. finishing step in the risotto method

D. Multiple Choice: For each question, choose the one correct answer.

1. When boiling potatoes you should add enough salt to the water to make it:
   a. slightly salty
   b. very salty
   c. medium salty
   d. not taste of salt at all

2. Fully cooked boiled potatoes can be easily pierced with:
   a. skewer
   b. paring knife
   c. tines of a fork
   d. all of the above

3. The most important point about making purées is that the potatoes should be _____ when you purée them.
   a. cold
   b. cool
   c. warm
   d. very hot

4. One piece of equipment that should not be used to purée potatoes is:
   a. a food processor
   b. a food mill
   c. a wooden spoon
   d. a potato masher

5. Before adding milk or cream to whipped potatoes it should be:
   a. chilled
   b. strained
   c. heated
   d. seasoned

6. Croquette and dauphine potatoes are examples of:
   a. roasted potatoes
   b. puréed potatoes
   c. deep-fried potatoes
   d. baked potatoes

E. True or False: Circle either True or False to indicate the correct answer.

1. Potatoes should be wrapped in foil before baking.

    True   False

2. Oven roasted potatoes are cooked in oil, butter, or rendered juices from a roasted item.

    True   False

3. Scalloped potatoes and au gratin potatoes are examples of puréed potatoes.

    True   False

4. French fries and steak fries as well as waffle-cut, matchstick, and soufflé potatoes are all deep-fried potatoes.

    True   False

5. Blanched fried potatoes have been cooked in oil heated to 375 degrees F to 400 degrees F until they are tender.

    True   False

6. To turn large potato cakes, use a spatula or long-handled spoon.

    True   False

7. When whole grains have finished cooking, stir them with a spoon to fluff them and release excess steam.

    True   False

8. Short grain rice is one of the most common grains to use for a pilaf.

    True   False

9. Heating the grain in hot fat or oil begins to gelatinize the starches.

    True   False

10. When a pilaf is properly cooked, the grains will separate easily.

    True   False

UNIT 26 ANSWER KEY

A. Terminology

All definitions can be found in the text.

B. Short Answer

1. a. Potatoes: all-purpose, new, waxy yellow
    b. Grains: rice, bulgur, barley
    c. Legumes: black beans, chick-peas, fava beans

2. a. An evenly soft, smooth texture
    b. Fully cooked but not falling apart
    c. Sweet, earthy flavor

3. a. Cream or milk—should be warmed
    b. Butter—should be at room temperature, but not melted
    c. Eggs—should be at room temperature

4. a. Scrub the potatoes.
    b. Blot them dry.
    c. Pierce them with a fork.

C. Matching

1. f
2. e
3. a
4. g
5. c
6. h
7. b
8. d

D. Multiple Choice

1. a
2. d
3. d
4. a
5. c
6. c

E. True or False

1. False
2. True
3. False
4. True
5. False
6. False
7. False
8. False
9. True
10. True

UNIT 27
BREAKFAST

A. Terminology: Fill in the blank space with the correct definition.

1. boiled _____

2. coddled _____

3. shirred _____

4. sunny-side up _____

5. over easy (medium, or hard) _____

6. scrambled _____

7. omelet _____

8. soufflé _____

9. quiche _____

10. crêpes _____

11. waffles _____

12. French toast _____

13. cereal _____

B. Fill in the Blank: Fill in the blank with the word that best completes the sentence.

1. Some batters for pancakes, crêpes, and waffles can be prepared up to

_____ ahead of time and held in the refrigerator.

2. Waffle batters are similar to pancakes batter, though they are slightly

_____.

3. Crepes are generally prepared in special _____.

4. When preparing crepe batter, the liquid should be at _____ temperature.

5. Crepe batter is the consistency of _____.

6. Cooked French toast can be held successfully for service for up to

   _____ minutes, after which the texture will start to decline.

7. When held in a steam table, hot cereals will _____.

8. Hash is a mixture of _____, _____, and

   _____.

C. Multiple Choice: For each question, choose the one correct answer.

1. When frying eggs, if the egg is not turned, it is referred to as:
   a. over easy
   b. sunny-side up
   c. over hard
   d. basted

2. Scrambled eggs are cooked over:
   a. low heat
   b. moderate heat
   c. moderately high heat
   d. very high heat

3. Rolled omelets are most commonly:
   a. made to order
   b. made in advance and reheated
   c. made in advance and kept hot for service
   d. made in advance and served at room temperature

4. Omelets cooked on a griddle are:
   a. rolled into an oval
   b. served in a square shape
   c. folded in half
   d. folded in thirds

5. A typical individual soufflé takes about _____ minutes to bake.
   a. 10
   b. 12
   c. 15
   d. 18

6. A soufflé base is made with a:
   a. velouté sauce
   b. béchamel sauce
   c. hollandaise sauce
   d. brown sauce

7. Typically, soufflés bake in ovens set at:
   a. 325 degrees F
   b. 350 degrees F
   c. 400 degrees F
   d. 425 degrees F

8. Waffles are typically cooked:
   a. in the oven
   b. on a griddle
   c. in a skillet
   d. on a waffle iron

D. True or False: Circle either True or False to indicate the correct answer.

1. The folds on a chef's hat represent the many ways he or she can prepare omelets.

   True   False

2. Hard-cooked eggs can be started in either boiling or cold water.

   True   False

3. Water at or close to a simmer cooks eggs evenly without toughening the whites.

   True   False

4. When baking eggs, the size, shape, and material of the baking dish has no affect on the texture of the finished item, or on the baking time.

   True   False

5. Eggs Benedict is a good example of a classic baked egg dish.

   True   False

6. When poaching eggs, a small amount of acid (vinegar) keeps the egg whites from spreading for attractive, regular shape.

       True   False

7. When evaluating the quality of poached eggs, the yolks should be thickened and not flowing.

       True   False

8. Frying is a typically French way of preparing and serving eggs.

       True   False

9. When frying eggs, if the heat is too low, the egg may stick to the griddle or sauté pan.

       True   False

10. Fried eggs should have broken yolks, cooked well done.

       True   False

UNIT 27 ANSWER KEY

A. Terminology

All definitions can be found in the text.

B. Fill in the Blank

1. one day
2. stiffer
3. pans
4. room
5. heavy cream
6. 30
7. continue to thicken
8. chopped cooked meats, potatoes, onions

C. Multiple Choice

1. b
2. b
3. a
4. c
5. d
6. b
7. d
8. d

D. True or False

1. False
2. True
3. True
4. False
5. False
6. True
7. False
8. False
9. True
10. False

UNIT 28
SALAD DRESSINGS AND SALADS

A. Terminology: Fill in the blank space with the correct definition.

1. dressing _____

2. vinaigrette _____

3. mayonnaise _____

4. emulsion _____

5. green salad _____

6. salad greens _____

7. croutons _____

8. composed salad _____

9. warm salad _____

10. vegetable salad _____

11. potato salad _____

12. legume salad _____

13. pasta salad _____

14. fruit salad _____

B. Short Answer: Provide a short response that correctly answers each of the questions below.

1. List the 3 basic types of salad dressings.

a. _____

b. _____

c. _____

2. List 4 guidelines for dairy-based dressings.

    a. _____

        _____

    b. _____

        _____

    c. _____

        _____

    d. _____

        _____

3. List the 4 steps in preparing the greens for a green salad.

    a. _____

        _____

    b. _____

        _____

    c. _____

        _____

    d. _____

        _____

4. List the 4 steps in preparing croutons.

    a. _____

        _____

    b. _____

        _____

c. _____

_____

d. _____

_____

C. Multiple Choice: For each question, choose the one correct answer.

1. In most circumstances, vinaigrettes are served:
   a. well chilled
   b. slightly chilled
   c. at room temperature
   d. warm

2. Mayonnaise:
   a. is the most stable of the basic salad dressings
   b. is the least stable of the basic salad dressings
   c. contains a higher ratio of vinegar to oil than is required for an emulsified vinaigrette
   d. contains less egg yolks than is required for an emulsified vinaigrette

3. In addition to sour cream, dairy-based dressings can contain:
   a. crème fraîche
   b. yogurt
   c. buttermilk
   d. all of the above

4. Salad dressings cling best to:
   a. washed greens, still wet
   b. washed and drip-dried greens, still moist
   c. washed and spin-dried greens, well-dried
   d. you should never wash salad greens

5. Generally, each portion of salad should get:
   a. 1–3 teaspoons of dressing
   b. 1–3 tablespoons of dressing
   c. 2–3 tablespoons of dressing
   d. 1/4 cup of salad dressing

6. Salad greens tossed with a hot dressing are known as:
   a. warm salads
   b. wilted salads
   c. salade tiède
   d. all of the above

7. Fruits that turn brown from oxidizing can be treated with:
   a. fruit juice
   b. milk
   c. stock
   d. vinegar

8. When making composed salads, one should:
   a. never repeat colors
   b. strive for a natural look
   c. toss the elements together
   d. take care to not add height to the salad

9. Composed salads are usually served as:
   a. an accompaniment only
   b. an appetizer
   c. a main course
   d. a main course or an appetizer

10. When washing salad greens, use a:
    a. sink filled with cool water
    b. sink filled with warm water
    c. colander, under cool running water
    d. colander, under warm running water

D. True or False: Circle either True or False to indicate the correct answer.

1. Composed salads are usually arranged on the plate, rather than tossing them together.

   True   False

2. The classic American potato salad is a creamy salad, dressed with vinaigrette.

   True   False

3. Pasta or grain salads have a tendency to become more flavorful as they sit.

   True   False

4. Unlike grains and pastas, which might become too soft as they sit in a dressing, beans will not soften any further.

   True   False

5. Fruits that turn brown (apples, pears, and bananas) can be treated with fruit juice to keep them from oxidizing, as long as the flavor of the juice doesn't compete with the other ingredients in the salad.

    True   False

6. Mixed fruit salads that include highly perishable fruits can be produced for volume operations by preparing the base from the most perishable fruits.

    True   False

7. The generally accepted ratio for a vinaigrette is three parts oil to one part vinegar.

    True   False

8. Mayonnaise is the least stable of the basic salad dressings.

    True   False

9. When making mayonnaise, have all the ingredients at the same temperature—room temperature—before preparation begins.

    True   False

10. Mayonnaise is sometimes included in a list of the grand sauces.

    True   False

UNIT 28 ANSWER KEY

A. Terminology

All definitions can be found in the text.

B. Short Answer

1. a. Vinaigrettes
   b. Mayonnaise-based
   c. Dairy-based

2. a. Keep dairy-based dressings refrigerated at all times.
   b. Check seasonings carefully before using.
   c. Add acidic ingredients such as lemon juice or vinegar to brighten the flavor.
   d. Make fresh batched as necessary for the best flavor.

3. a. Wash the greens thoroughly in plenty of cool water to remove all traces of dirt or sand.
   b. Dry the greens completely.
   c. Store the cleaned greens in tubs or other containers.
   d. Cut or tear the lettuce into bite-sized pieces.

4. a. Cut the bread into the desired size.
   b. Rub, spray, brush, or toss the cubes or slices lightly with olive oil or clarified butter, if appropriate.
   c. Add the salt and pepper and other flavorings as desired.
   d. Spread the croutons in a single layer on a sheet pan and toast in a moderate oven until golden, turning them from time to time.

C. Multiple Choice

   1. c
   2. a
   3. d
   4. c
   5. c
   6. d
   7. a
   8. b
   9. d
   10. a

D. True or False

1. True
2. False
3. False
4. True
5. True
6. False
7. True
8. False
9. True
10. True

UNIT 29
SANDWICHES

A. Terminology: Fill in the blank space with the correct definition.

1. open-faced sandwiches _____

2. club sandwich _____

3. griddled sandwich _____

4. finger or tea sandwich _____

5. bread _____

6. spread _____

7. filling _____

8. garnish _____

B. Fill in the Blank: Fill in the blank with the word that best completes the sentence.

1. Coarsely grained or peasant-style breads are good for

   _____ sandwiches served as a _____

   menu item.

2. Wrappers (plain or flavored wraps, wheat tortillas, and similar flexible

   flatbreads) are featured in special sandwiches, especially those featured in -

   _____ or _____ cuisines.

3. Lettuce leaves, slices of tomato or onion, sprouts, marinated or brined

   peppers, and olives are just a few of the many ingredients that can be used to

   _____ sandwiches.

4. The best sandwiches are made from high quality ingredients that are

   _____ handled.

5. Filling ingredients for club sandwiches need to be at the correct

   _____.

6. Club sandwiches are cut into _____ before serving.

7. When producing finger and tea sandwiches, un-sliced

   _____ loaves can be sliced lengthwise to speed production

   and increase yield.

8. When producing sandwiches, organize your _____

   carefully to be as efficient as possible.

C. Short Answer: Provide a short response that correctly answers each of the
   questions below.

   1. What are 4 types of rolls used in sandwiches?

      a. _____

      b. _____

      c. _____

      d. _____

   2. List 4 spreads other than the classical sandwich spreads.

      a. _____

      b. _____

      c. _____

      d. _____

3. List 5 different types of fillings used in sandwiches.

a. _____

b. _____

c. _____

d. _____

e. _____

D. True or False: Circle either True or False to indicate the correct answer.

1. The characteristics of the bread and how it will fit in with the sandwiches should not be considered.

       True   False

2. Most breads cannot be sliced in advance of sandwich preparation.

       True   False

3. Toasting should be done only immediately before assembling the sandwich.

       True   False

4. Some sandwich fillings have the spread directly in the filling mixture (for example, a mayonnaise-dressed tuna salad); still, there is a need to add another spread when assembling the sandwich.

       True   False

5. The filling determines how all the other elements of the sandwich are selected and prepared.

       True   False

6. Garnishes become part of the sandwich's overall structure.

       True   False

7. A club sandwich calls for a flatbread that is toasted as closely as possible to the time you assemble and serve the sandwich.

        True   False

8. Finger and tea sandwiches are typically made in volume, so it is especially important to be organized as you start your work.

        True   False

UNIT 29 ANSWER KEY

A. Terminology

All definitions can be found in the text.

B. Fill in the Blank

1. larger, main
2. regional, ethnic
3. garnish
4. carefully
5. temperature
6. quarters
7. Pullman
8. workstation

C. Short Answer

1. a. Hard rolls
   b. Soft rolls
   c. Submarine or hoagie rolls
   d. Kaiser rolls

2. a. Spreadable cheeses
   b. Vegetable herb spreads
   c. Nut butters
   d. Guacamole

3. a. Sliced roasted or simmered meats (beef, corned beef, pastrami, turkey, ham, pâtés, sausages)
   b. Sliced cheeses
   c. Grilled, roasted, marinated, or fresh vegetables
   d. Grilled, pan-fried, or broiled burgers, sausages, fish, poultry, or eggs
   e. Salads of meats, poultry, eggs, fish, or vegetables

D. True or False

1. False
2. False
3. True
4. False
5. True
6. True
7. False
8. True

UNIT 30
HORS D'OEUVRES AND APPETIZERS

A. Terminology: Fill in the blank space with the correct definition.

1. hors d'oeuvres _____

2. appetizer _____

3. canapé _____

4. caviar _____

5. finger foods _____

6. crudité _____

7. mezze _____

8. tapas _____

9. antipasto _____

10. hors d'oeuvre variées _____

B. Fill in the Blank: Fill in the blank with the word that best completes the sentence.

1. The term "hors d'oeuvres" translates literally from the French as

   _____.

2. Hors d'oeuvres are meant to pique the _____ and perk up

   the _____.

3. With very few exceptions, hors d'oeuvres should not require a guest to use a

   _____.

4. Because hors d'oeuvres customarily precede the meal, they should be

   considered a means of _____ the _____.

5. The types of hors d'oeuvres that can be prepared and served by an

   establishment should be tailored to suit the needs and abilities of the

   _____ and _____ staffs and to the nature

   of the _____.

6. A traditional canapé includes a _____, often cut into

   shapes, a _____, a _____, and a

   _____.

7. Perfect canapés call for attention to _____.

8. Include two or more hot hors d'oeuvres in a reception menu to give the

   impression of _____.

9. To ensure that these hors d'oeuvres stay hot, do not combine hot and cold

   appetizers on a _____.

10. Hors d'oeuvre variés is a French tradition, usually served as part of a

    _____ menu. The guest makes selections from an offering

    of a variety of hot and cold hors d'oeuvres, often presented in dishes known as

    _____.

C. Multiple Choice: For each question, choose the one correct answer.

   1. The range of foods and cooking techniques suited to preparing hors d'oeuvres,
      appetizers, and salads is limited only:
      a. by the chef's imagination
      b. by the seasonal availability of produce
      c. by the general dictates of a particular menu
      d. all of the above

2. Finger foods are the natural choice for such occasions as:
   a. outdoor receptions
   b. sit-down dinners
   c. brunches
   d. formal luncheons

3. Canapé is a term often used to refer to a variety of:
   a. main course items
   b. hors d'oeuvres
   c. appetizers
   d. desserts

4. Some types of cold hors d'oeuvres are actually served:
   a. frozen
   b. heated
   c. at room temperature
   d. on warm plates

5. To hold hot hors d'oeuvres for buffet service, use:
   a. heated sauté pans
   b. trays with dollies
   c. chafing dishes
   d. warmed plates

6. Russians are famous for their:
   a. Mezze
   b. Zakuski
   c. Antojitos
   d. Tapas

7. Caviar is made from:
   a. fish roe
   b. salted cod
   c. puréed sturgeon
   d. smoked salmon

8. A popular way to serve caviar is:
   a. in a large bowl set in ice
   b. on a blini
   c. mixed with hard-cooked eggs
   d. blended with chopped onions and fresh lemon juice

9. Garnishes for appetizers should always be:
   a. warmed
   b. seasoned lightly
   c. edible
   d. picked for their color alone

10. Cold hors d'oeuvres are typically eaten:
    a. with the fingers
    b. with a hot sauce
    c. with a garnish of caviar
    d. with a fork

D. True or False: Circle either True or False to indicate the correct answer.

1. Hors d'oeuvres and appetizers are served before the meal or as its first course.

    True   False

2. In order to use many of the recipes learned in previous chapters to create hors d'oeuvres and appetizers, many of the ingredients, along with the portion size would need to be adjusted.

    True   False

3. Hors d'oeuvres can be served cold or hot.

    True   False

4. When preparing hors d'oeuvres, foods should be cooked carefully, and the appropriate standards for doneness, flavor, and appearance should be followed.

    True   False

5. With very few exceptions, hors d'oeuvres should require the guest to use a knife.

    True   False

6. Hot hors d'oeuvres may require a plate and a fork, skewers, or picks.

    True   False

7. The types of hors d'oeuvres that can be prepared and served by an establishment should be tailored to suit the needs and abilities of the kitchen and dining room staffs and to the nature of the event.

    True   False

8. Finger foods are the natural choice for occasions where the guests will be seated.

    True   False

9. Vegetables for crudités should be served well chilled.

        True   False

10. Canapés are a basic offering at most receptions.

        True   False

UNINT 30 ANSWER KEY

A. Terminology

All definitions can be found in the text.

B. Fill in the Blank

1. outside the work
2. taste buds, appetite
3. knife
4. teasing, appetite
5. kitchen, dining room, event
6. bread base, spread, filling, garnish
7. detail
8. substance
9. single platter, luncheon, raviers

C. Multiple Choice

1. d
2. a
3. b
4. c
5. c
6. b
7. a
8. b
9. c
10. a

D. True or False

1. True
2. False
3. True
4. True
5. False
6. True
7. True
8. False
9. True
10. True

UNIT 31
GARDE-MANGER

A. Terminology: Fill in the blank space with the correct definition.

1. garde-manger _____

2. forcemeat _____

3. emulsion _____

4. progressive grinding _____

5. panada _____

6. aspic gelée _____

7. straight forcemeat _____

8. country-style forcemeat _____

9. gratin forcemeat _____

10. mousseline forcemeat _____

11. dominant meat (theme meat) _____

12. pâté en croûte _____

13. cap piece _____

14. chimney_____

15. galantine _____

16. terrine _____

17. quenelles _____

18. dry cure _____

19. brine _____

20. gravadlax _____

B. Fill in the Blank: Fill in the blank with the word that best completes the sentence.

1. The top layer of a Pâté en croûte is called the _____.

2. When preparing a Pâté en croûte, save dough scraps to make the

   _____.

3. Roulades are rolled in a casing of _____ or

   _____ to produce a round shape.

4. Galantines should be cooled directly in the _____.

5. Curing salmon may be accomplished by using a _____ or a

   _____.

6. When preparing salmon for curing, the _____ and

   _____ should be removed, and the

   _____ left on.

7. To achieve the correct consistency when preparing fish or poultry forcemeat

   use a _____ instead of a meat grinder.

8. In some forcemeats, the _____ naturally present in the meat

   are enough to bind the forcemeat so that it slices well after it is cooked.

9. A binder should contribute no more than _____ percent of

   the forcemeat's total volume, excluding any garnish ingredients.

10. Aspic gelée is frequently strengthened by adding a quantity of

   _____.

208

C. Multiple Choice: For each question, choose the one correct answer.

1. The correct ratio of lean meat to fat is typically found in:
   a. chicken breasts
   b. pork butt
   c. veal shanks
   d. beef round

2. When making forcemeat, salt adds flavor and assists in creating:
   a. a good color
   b. better keeping qualities
   c. a good bind
   d. a better emulsification

3. For the first pass in progressive grinding, you should use:
   a. a fine die
   b. a medium die
   c. a course die
   d. a food processor

4. Pâtés and terrines are:
   a. poached
   b. sautéed
   c. grilled
   d. baked

5. So that it can be sliced easily, a country-style forcemeat usually includes:
   a. a binder
   b. a garnish
   c. a pâté dough
   d. seared liver

6. A mousseline forcemeat has a:
   a. light texture
   b. medium texture
   c. course texture
   d. chunky texture

7. Terrines are:
   a. casings stuffed with forcemeat
   b. loaves of forcemeat
   c. quenelles
   d. cured forcemeats

8. The term galantine derives from an old French word meaning:
   a. stuffed
   b. formed
   c. chicken
   d. baked

9. A galantine is traditionally wrapped in:
   a. a casing of cheesecloth
   b. tin-foil
   c. plastic wrap
   d. poultry skin

10. Pâté en croûte is made by baking a forcemeat in:
    a. a pastry lined mold
    b. a casing
    c. poultry skin
    d. cheesecloth

D. True or False: Circle either True or False to indicate the correct answer.

1. The term Garde-Manger has only one meaning; translated from the French, it means, "keep to eat."

   True   False

2. A forcemeat is an emulsion produced by grinding lean meat and fat together.

   True   False

3. Some forcemeats can be shaped into dumplings, known in French as galantines.

   True   False

4. When making forcemeats, maintaining the correct temperature is important for more than the proper formation of an emulsion.

   True   False

5. When preparing forcemeats, meats should be cut cleanly, never mangled or mashed, as they pass through the grinder.

   True   False

6. Pâte à choux is sometimes used as a binder when preparing forcemeat.

   True   False

7. Pâté dough is a weaker dough than ordinary pie dough.

        True   False

8. When preparing forcemeat, the dominant meat (including fish, chicken, or vegetable) should be the dominating flavor.

        True   False

9. Seasonings are more pronounced in cold foods.

        True   False

10. Most forcemeat preparations are served hot.

        True   False

UNIT 31 ANSWER KEY

A. Terminology

    All definitions can be found in the text.

B. Fill in the Blank

    1. cap piece
    2. chimney
    3. cheesecloth, plastic
    4. cooking liquid
    5. dry cure, wet cure
    6. pin bones, belly flap, skin
    7. food processor
    8. proteins
    9. 20
    10. gelatin

C. Multiple Choice

    1. b
    2. c
    3. c
    4. d
    5. a
    6. a
    7. b
    8. c
    9. d
    10. a

D. True or False

    1. False
    2. True
    3. False
    4. True
    5. True
    6. True
    7. False
    8. True
    9. False
    10. False

A. Terminology: Fill in the blank space with the correct definition.

1. proofing _____

2. first rise (bulk fermentation) _____

3. well mixing method _____

4. sifting _____

5. scaling (ingredients as well as batters or doughs) _____

_____

6. quickbread _____

7. rubbed dough method _____

8. blind baking _____

9. docking _____

10. pâte à choux _____

11. creaming method _____

12. stirred custard _____

13. tempering _____

14. baked custard _____

15. pastry cream _____

16. Bavarian cream _____

B. Fill in the Blank: Fill in the blank with the word that best completes the sentence.

1. Among the most common uses for Pâte á choux are _____,

_____, and _____.

2. When preparing Pâte á choux, the batter is cooked over medium heat, stirring

   constantly, until the mixture _____ from the pan and forms

   a _____.

3. Baked Pâte á choux shells should be _____ with a dry,

   delicate _____.

4. Pâte à choux is made by combining _____,

   _____, _____, and

   _____ into a smooth batter.

5. _____ can be substituted for water in the production of Pâte

   á choux.

6. When producing Pâte á choux the liquid and butter is brought to a

   _____ boil and then the _____ are added

   all at once.

C. Short Answer: Provide a short response that correctly answers each of the
   questions below.

   1. List 3 guidelines for evaluating the quality of yeast breads.

      a. _____

         _____

      b. _____

         _____

      c. _____

         _____

2. List 3 guidelines for proofing yeasts.

   a. _____

   _____

   b. _____

   _____

   c. _____

   _____

3. List the 3 steps in preparing a pre-baked pie shell, or "blind baking."

   a. _____

   _____

   b. _____

   _____

   c. _____

   _____

D. Multiple Choice: For each question, choose the one correct answer.

   1. The well mixing method calls for the dry ingredients and the wet ingredients
      to be:
      a. combined one dry and one wet ingredient at a time
      b. combined all at once
      c. combined in two steps
      d. combined in three steps

   2. Pâte à choux is made by combining water, butter, flour, and _____ into a
      smooth batter.
      a. whole eggs
      b. egg yolks
      c. egg whites
      d. dried eggs

3. Pâte à choux items are first baked at:
   a. 300 degrees F–325 degrees F
   b. 325 degrees F–350 degrees F
   c. 350 degrees F–375 degrees F
   d. 375 degrees F–400 degrees F

4. The interior of cookies and cakes made by the creaming method should be moist with a uniform, even grain and:
   a. no large holes
   b. no golden edges
   c. no golden bottoms
   d. no crispy exterior

5. Custards cooked over direct heat are referred to as:
   a. baked custards
   b. poached custards
   c. stirred custards
   d. simmered custards

6. The flavor and color of vanilla sauce is determined by:
   a. high temperatures
   b. quick cooking
   c. the amount of sugar used
   d. quality ingredients

7. Soufflés are typically baked in individual molds that have been:
   a. brushed with softened butter
   b. lined with paper
   c. preheated
   d. dusted with flour

8. One of the most popular mousse flavors is:
   a. vanilla
   b. strawberry
   c. coffee
   d. chocolate

E. True or False: Circle either True or False to indicate the correct answer.

1. Begin mixing yeast doughs on medium speed.

         True   False

2. Folding the yeast dough over on itself is done to expel the carbon dioxide, even out the temperature, and redistribute the yeast evenly.

         True   False

3. If there is any doubt about whether or not the yeast is still alive, it should be "proofed" before it is added to the other ingredients.

     True   False

4. The basic skills involved in making any yeast-raised bread, from mixing and kneading to proofing and shaping, are skills that only bakers need to develop.

     True   False

5. Pie dough is easier to roll out right after being kneaded.

     True   False

6. Custard-type fillings should be carefully poured into the shell to the rim of the pan.

     True   False

7. A lattice crust is made by cutting strips of dough, and laying them on the top of the dough to make a grid.

     True   False

8. Meringue topping is slowly browned in a moderately hot oven.

     True   False

9. For a double-crusted pie, brush the top crust very lightly with egg wash and bake the pie on a sheet pan in a hot oven (425degrees F/205degrees C) until done.

     True   False

10. The texture of piecrust is determined in large part by the mixing method.

     True   False

UNIT 32 ANSWER KEY

A. Terminology

All definitions can be found in the text.

B. Fill in the Blank

1. cream puffs, profiteroles, éclairs
2. pulls away, ball
3. hollow, texture
4. water, butter, flour, eggs
5. milk
6. rolling, dry ingredients

C. Short Answer

1. a. Properly baked rolls and loaves have a rich aroma and golden to brown color.
   b. Baguettes should not split open if they are scored before baking.
   c. The grain should be open and the texture firm.

2. a. Combine the yeast with the room temperature liquid and a small amount of the flour or sugar
   b. Let the mixture rest at room temperature until a thick foam forms on the surface.
   c. The foam indicates that the yeast is alive and can be used. If there is no foam, the yeast is dead and should be discarded.

3. a. The dough is prepared, rolled out, and fitted into the pan.
   b. The dough is pierced in several places with the tines of a fork (known as docking) to prevent blisters from forming in the dough as it bakes.
   c. The pastry is then covered with parchment paper and filled with pie weights or dried beans before baking the crust.

D. Multiple Choice

1. b
2. a
3. d
4. a
5. c
6. d
7. a
8. d

E. True or False

1. False
2. True
3. True
4. False
5. False
6. False
7. True
8. False
9. True
10. True

FLAVOR DEVELOPMENT

A. Terminology: Fill in the blank space with the correct definition.

1. flavor _____

2. seasoning _____

3. aroma _____

4. bitter _____

5. sour _____

6. salty _____

7. umami _____

8. texture _____

9. flavor profile _____

B. Fill in the Blank: Fill in the blank with the word that best completes the sentence.

1. Aromatic combinations such as _____,

_____, _____, the

_____ trinity, and _____ provide the

base flavors that identify a regional style of cooking.

2. Cured or smoked foods can be used to add a distinctive

_____ to a dish.

3. A food's overall flavor profile can range from _____ to

_____.

4. The term flavor profile refers to the _____ widely used to

season many dishes in a given _____.

5. The temperature at which foods are served affects our ability to perceive

   _____.

6. The amount of time that a flavor lingers on the palate of the taster after the

   food has been swallowed will influence the _____ of the

   overall flavor.

7. The act of tasting foods properly should draw upon all of the chefs

   _____.

8. Fruits, vegetables, and herbs can be tasted _____ safely.

9. Meats, eggs, poultry, and mixtures that contain potentially hazardous foods

   should be _____ before tasting.

10. To keep foods cooked in batches safe, use tasting spoons and be sure that you

   do not _____ the tasting spoons.

C. Matching: Match each of the terms in List A with the appropriate description in
   List B.

List A	*List B*
___1. smell	a. *On Food and Cooking*
___2. mouthfeel	b. crystal clear
___3. opaque	c. how foods feel
___4. translucent	d. onions, celery, lemons, ginger
___5. transparent	e. used to enhance and develop flavor in foods
___6. consommé	f. some light will pass through

___7. salt   g. light does not pass through

___8. stems of fresh herbs   h. fragrance or aroma

___9. aromatics   i. clear

___10. Harold McGee   j. component of sachets and bouquet garn

D. Multiple Choice: For each question, choose the one correct answer.

1. Salt as well as foods cured in salt give foods:
   a. an ivory color on the outside
   b. a tough interior
   c. a salty flavor
   d. a sour flavor

2. When a food that should be firm feels soft, we describe the food as:
   a. properly cooked
   b. underdone
   c. overdone
   d. dry

3. Foods that stiffen as they cook, include those that are:
   a. fried
   b. braised
   c. stewed
   d. boiled

4. Foods that lighten as they cook include foods that are:
   a. lightened with steam
   b. lightened with a foam
   c. lightened with a leavener
   d. all of the above

5. Salt has the ability to bring out a foods natural flavor when added:
   a. in low levels
   b. in large amounts
   c. at the end of the cooking time
   d. at the table by the guest

6. Salt enhances:
   a. sour flavors
   b. bitter flavors
   c. metallic flavors
   d. sweet flavors

7. Mincing or shredding herbs:
   a. releases more of their flavor
   b. diminishes their flavor
   c. is seldom done by the chef
   d. is done at least one hour before use

8. Grinding spices releases more flavor and should be done:
   a. in small batches
   b. in large batches
   c. before they are toasted
   d. one day in advance

E. True or False: Circle either True or False to indicate the correct answer.

1. Flavor is the word we use to indicate only one aspect of a dish.

   True   False

2. Flavor is a complex experience and one that is difficult to describe in concrete and objective terms.

   True   False

3. Taste is the word we use to indicate the total experience of a dish.

   True   False

4. The terms we use to describe our food experiences, taste, texture, aroma, color, and even its sound, have become the language of food quality.

   True   False

5. Soy sauces, including light, dark, and tamari, add a savory flavor, referred to in Japanese as umami.

   True   False

6. Aroma, pungent, and earthy are descriptive words that pertain to the way foods smell.

   True   False

7. When foods are properly paired with a technique, the flavor of the ingredients is developed even further.

   True   False

8. Generally, as foods cook their appearance does not change.

        True   False

9. A poached chicken breast is an ivory color on the inside and a dark mahogany on the outside.

        True   False

10. Texture changes during the cooking process are an important way to gauge how well done a food is.

        True   False

UNIT 33 ANSWER KEY

A. Terminology

All definitions can be found in the text.

B. Fill in the Blank

1. mirepoix, matignon, bouquet garni, Cajun, sofrito
2. aroma
3. simple, complex
4. seasonings, cuisine
5. tastes
6. perception
7. senses
8. raw
9. cooked
10. reuse

C. Matching

1. h
2. c
3. g
4. f
5. i
6. b
7. e
8. j
9. d
10. a

D. Multiple Choice

1. c
2. b
3. a
4. d
5. a
6. d
7. a
8. a

E. True or False

1. False
2. True
3. False
4. True
5. True
6. True
7. True
8. False
9. False
10. True

UNIT 34
PLATING AND PRESENTATION

A. Terminology: Fill in the blank space with the correct definition.

1. presentation _____

2. symmetrical _____

3. asymmetrical _____

4. saucing techniques _____

5. functional and nonfunctional garnishes _____

   _____

6. focal point _____

7. lines _____

8. patterns _____

B. Fill in the Blank: Fill in the blank with the word that best completes the sentence.

1. Presenting foods properly calls upon the chef to consider the foods natural

   _____.

2. Good presentation begins with good _____.

3. We eat with our eyes _____.

4. The four categories of elements that can appear on a plate of food are the

   _____, _____, _____,

   and _____.

5. Symmetrical presentations often give the impression of

   _____ and _____.

6. When contrasting elements appear near each other, they throw each other into

    _____, each one making the other

    _____.

7. A focal point draws your _____.

8. The focal point may be any of the basic _____ on the plate.

9. For plating and presentation, the most adaptable shaped plate is a

    _____ plate with a _____.

10. Large plates give a look of _____ and

    _____, as long as the plate is not so big that the food begins

    to look _____.

11. Trying to fit too much onto a small plate results in a _____

    or _____ presentation.

12. Dishes like rice pilaf, spaghetti, or casseroled potatoes can be

    _____, _____, or

    _____ to give them a neat, attractive shape.

C. Multiple Choice: For each question, choose the one correct answer.

1. Presentations that give the impression of formality are:
   a. symmetrical
   b. asymmetrical
   c. complementary
   d. uncomplementary

2. In a plate presentation, a focal point:
    a. is always centered
    b. is never centered
    c. draws your attention
    d. does not use any of the basic elements on the plate

3. To give the impression of motion, use:
    a. lines that radiate from a central point
    b. lines that are curved
    c. lines that are not exactly the same length
    d. all of the above

4. All plates, bowls, and serving pieces should be:
    a. made of porcelain
    b. meticulously clean
    c. round and have a rim
    d. square and have a design or logo on them

5. When arranging food on a plate, whenever possible you should:
    a. avoid wasted space by covering the rim with food
    b. avoid using natural colors as a guide
    c. avoid filling the plate completely
    d. avoid creating a focal point with colors or height

6. Garnishes should:
    a. be edible
    b. serve a function beyond simply adding color
    c. be positioned for maximum effect
    d. all of the above

7. When arranging foods on a buffet, you should:
    a. keep hot foods near one another
    b. avoid displaying chilled foods
    c. place sauces and condiments in their own area
    d. keep foods that might spill furthest from the guests

8. Opinions concerning what is fashionable in plate presentation:
    a. never change
    b. are objective, not subjective
    c. change over time
    d. never happen overnight

D. True or False: Circle either True or False to indicate the correct answer.

1. Presentation is the art of telling our guests about the food by the way it is arranged on a serving piece.

    True   False

2. An effective presentation focuses on the entrée, and not the side dishes, sauces, or garnishes.

    True   False

3. Asymmetrical presentations are sometimes described as unnatural.

    True   False

4. Trying to fit too much onto a small plate results in a messy or jumbled presentation.

    True   False

5. Large cuts of meat or fish can be plated without being sliced or cut in order to give the impression of a more generous portion.

    True   False

6. In order to preserve the texture of foods with crisp crusts, ladle sauces over the items and not under or around them.

    True   False

7. Choosing the right garnish requires less care and thought than choosing the seasonings and aromatics for the dish.

    True   False

8. Patterns are the result of repeating a shape, a line, a color, or a flavor over and over again.

    True   False

UNIT 34 ANSWER KEY

A. Terminology

All definitions can be found in the text.

B. Fill in the Blank

1. characteristics
2. technique
3. first
4. main item, side dishes, sauces, garnishes
5. formality, stillness
6. relief, stand out
7. attention
8. elements
9. round, rim
10. elegance, richness, skimpy
11. messy, jumbled
12. molded, scooped, cut

C. Multiple Choice

1. a
2. c
3. d
4. b
5. c
6. d
7. a
8. c

D. True or False

1. True
2. False
3. False
4. True
5. False
6. False
7. False
8. True

UNIT 35
THE COOKING OF EUROPE AND THE MEDITERRANEAN

A. Terminology: Fill in the blank space with the correct definition.

1. classical cooking _____

2. bitter greens _____

3. herbs _____

4. Ottoman Empire _____

5. Persian Empire _____

6. Mahgreb _____

7. Iberian Peninsula _____

B. Fill in the Blank: Fill in the blank with the word that best completes the sentence.

1. Classical cooking got its start in _____ and has become the standard for evaluating professional cooking.

2. French classical cooking has been regarded as one of the leading cuisines in most restaurants, due to the influence of Chef _____.

3. The cooking in northern Italy is as likely to use _____ as oil or to replace wheat-based pastas with _____.

4. In the south of France, _____, a thick paste made from olives, anchovies, capers and olive oil), and _____ (anchovies softened in olive oil, with finely chopped garlic) are often served on toasted or grilled breads.

5. Oysters, mussels, and monkfish are among the most popular ingredients in the

_____ region of France.

6. In the center of France (Lyonnaise, Franche-Comté, Savoie, Dauphiné,

Bourgogne, Auvergne, Limousin, and Loire-Atlantique),

_____ is an important part of the economy as well as in the

cuisine.

7. Burgundy, France, is known for its fine _____ and Bresse

is renowned for its _____.

8. Italy consists of a long, narrow peninsula with a mountainous interior and

plenty of _____.

9. In Sicily, the food is _____ and _____

and often flavored with pungent herbs such as basil, oregano, marjoram, and

rosemary.

10. In northern Italy, _____ is typically replaced by

_____.

C. Short Answer: Provide a short response that correctly answers each of the
   questions below.

1. List 3 food specialties of Périgord, a region in Southwestern France.

   a. _____

   b. _____

   c. _____

2. List the 3 types of livestock raised in the mountainous passes of Spain that border the Mediterranean.

   a. _____

   b. _____

   c. _____

3. List 3 condiments that the British Empire introduced and popularized to Western diners.

   a. _____

   b. _____

   c. _____

4. List the 3 countries that comprise central Europe.

   a. _____

   b. _____

   c. _____

D. True or False: Circle either True or False to indicate the correct answer.

1. In the north of Eastern Europe (Russian, Poland, and Hungary), rye is the main cereal crop.

   True   False

2. Turnips are the foundation of a soup served throughout Eastern Europe—known as borscht in Russia.

   True   False

3. The countries of Eastern Europe (Russian, Poland, and Hungary) are often credited as being the birthplace of civilization.

   True   False

4. Cheeses and yogurt made from sheep and goat's milk are a prominent feature throughout the Eastern Mediterranean countries.

        True   False

5. The North African coastline, although part of the African continent, shares a similar geography, climate, and culture with the rest of the Mediterranean.

        True   False

6. French classical cooking has been regarded as one of the leading cuisines in most restaurants.

        True   False

7. In the Eastern Mediterranean, flatbreads such as pita are often prepared daily in order to make fattoush, a bread salad.

        True   False

8. Morocco, Tunisia, and Algeria make up the Ottoman Empire.

        True   False

UNIT 35 ANSWER KEY

A. Terminology

All definitions can be found in the text.

B. Fill in the Blank

1. France
2. Auguste Escoffier
3. butter, rice
4. tapenade, anchoïade
5. Southwestern
6. cheesemaking
7. beef cattle, poultry
8. coastline
9. hot, spicy
10. olive oil, butter

C. Short Answer

1. a. Truffles
    b. Duck confit
    c. Foie gras

2. a. Cattle
    b. Sheep
    c. Goats

3. a. Ketchup
    b. Chutney
    c. Worcestershire sauce

4. a. Switzerland
    b. Austria
    c. Germany

D. True or False

1. True
2. False
3. False
4. True
5. True
6. True
7. False
8. False

A. Terminology: Fill in the blank space with the correct definition.

1. stir fry _____

2. wok _____

3. soy sauce _____

4. fish sauce _____

5. rice _____

6. curries _____

B. Fill in the Blank: Fill in the blank with the word that best completes the sentence.

1. In Japan, _____ is prepared by frying a wide range of foods

   after they are coated in a light batter; this technique was most likely

   introduced to Japan by the _____.

2. In Asian cuisine, salads are served as _____ and

   _____, sometimes used as a way to cool the heat in other

   dishes or cleanse the palate.

3. In _____ Asia, grilled satays of skewered meats, fish, or

   poultry, are served with a _____ sauce.

4. There are distinct styles of curry found throughout Asia, especially in

   Southeast Asia, where they often include _____, and India,

   where they often include _____.

5. The great Achievement of Asian cuisines is the _____,

even _____, approach to food and cooking that stresses the

importance of _____ and _____ foods in

both a dish and in the structure of a meal.

C. Matching: Match each of the terms in List A with the appropriate word, definition, or description in List B.

List A	*List B*
____1. wok	a. pickled cabbage
____2. China	b. used for stewing and braising
____3. Beijing	c. type of horseradish
____4. Japan	d. basmati rice
____5. wasabi	e. Kaffir lime leaves
____6. Thailand	f. Kobe beef
____7. kimchee	g. Northern China
____8. India	h. a round-bottomed
____9. durian	i. The Great Wall
____10. clay pots with lids	j. a type of fruit found in Asia

D. Multiple Choice: For each question, choose the one correct answer.

1. Asian cooking is often described as striving toward:
   a. a balance of flavors
   b. a balance of colors
   c. a spicy flavor
   d. a sweet flavor

2. Much of Asian cuisine has been influenced at one time or another by:
   a. the Japanese
   b. the Chinese
   c. the Vietnamese
   d. the Koreans

3. Hindus considered what animal sacred?
   a. the horse
   b. the cow
   c. the goat
   d. the pig

4. Dim sum, stir fries made with seafood and poultry, and rich sauces are part of this cuisine's makeup.
   a. Szechwan
   b. Beijing
   c. Fujian
   d. Canton

5. Hot and spicy, and hot and sour flavor combinations are popular in this Chinese cuisine.
   a. Beijing
   b. Hunan
   c. Fujian
   d. Canton

6. In Japanese cuisine raw seafood is called:
   a. sushi
   b. wasabi
   c. kobe
   d. sashimi

7. The only country in Southeast Asia that uses chopsticks is:
   a. Thailand
   b. Korea
   c. Vietnam
   d. Malaysia

8. A form of clarified butter used in India is called:
   a. ghee
   b. masala
   c. cassia
   d. naan

E. True or False: Circle either True or False to indicate the correct answer.

1. Beans, especially soybeans, are used widely throughout Asia.

   True   False

2. Okra, which arrived from China, is another common vegetable in Asia.

   True   False

3. Mushrooms are not an important feature in Asian cooking.

    True   False

4. In most parts of Asia, meat is used primarily as a main ingredient.

    True   False

5. Japan is famous for its raw seafood and fish dishes, known as sashimi.

    True   False

6. Dried and preserved fish are used as a seasoning ingredient and are often part
    of a rich broth used both as a cooking medium and a seasoning.

    True   False

7. Asian cooks employ a narrow array of ingredients but a wide range of
    techniques.

    True   False

8. In Asia, each region has a distinct flavor profile.

    True   False

9. Stir fried dishes are prepared by cutting foods in advance to shorten their
    cooking time and then, they are cooked slowly in a special cooking vessel.

    True   False

10. Deep-frying is a popular cooking technique in some parts of Asia.

    True   False

UNIT 36 ANSWER KEY

A. Terminology

All definitions can be found in the text.

B. Fill in the Blank

1. tempura, Portuguese
2. condiments, relishes
3. Southeast, peanut
4. coconut milk, yogurt
5. practical, frugal, balancing, harmonizing

C. Matching

1. h
2. i
3. g
4. f
5. c
6. e
7. a
8. d
9. j
10. b

D. Multiple Choice

1. a
2. b
3. b
4. d
5. b
6. d
7. c
8. a

E. True or False

1. True
2. False
3. False
4. False

5. True
6. True
7. False
8. True
9. False
10. True

UNIT 37
CUISINES OF THE AMERICAS

A. Terminology: Fill in the blank space with the correct definition.

1. three sisters _____

2. New England states _____

3. Mid-Atlantic states _____

4. scrapple _____

5. Gulf states _____

6. soul food _____

7. Cajun cuisine _____

8. Creole cuisine _____

9. Southwest states _____

10. Tex-Mex _____

11. Pacific states _____

12. cioppino _____

13. Carribean islands _____

14. jerk _____

15. Northern Mexico _____

16. Central Mexico _____

17. Southern Mexico _____

18. recados _____

19. moles_____

20. Central America _____

21. ceviche _____

22. escabeche_____

B. Fill in the Blank: Fill in the blank with the word that best completes the sentence.

1. When Christopher Columbus and other explorers arrived in the Western Hemisphere, there were already were established and advanced societies in some areas, notably the _____, _____, and _____ cultures.

2. The arrival of the _____ and the _____ in South America and the _____ and _____ in North America established cooking styles that we associate with those regions.

3. Corn was probably first raised in the _____ area of Mexico.

4. When eaten with _____, beans provide excellent nourishment.

5. Foods in the Americas prior to the Europeans' arrival were cooked over or near _____, wrapped in leaves and steamed in _____, or cooked on _____ similar to griddles.

6. Europeans introduced cookware made from _____.

7. Asian settlers introduced the _____ and _____.

244

8. Central America is a narrow _____ connecting North and South America.

9. The cooking of Peru and surrounding countries is often described as having two components: the cooking _____ and the cooking _____.

10. In _____, the combination of black bean and white rice, sprinkled with manioc meal (an indigenous starchy root crop), is eaten at least once a day.

C. Matching: Match each of the terms in List A with the appropriate word, definition, or description in List B.

List A	List B
___1. American Cuisine	a. jerk
___2. frying in oil	b. grits, hominy, collard greens
___3. chowder crackers	c. cioppino
___4. Southwestern United States	d. a traditional preparation of the Pacific States
___5. Fisherman's Wharf	e. unique to New England
___6. Carribean barbeque	f. today's most popular regional cuisine
___7. pumpkin seeds	g. cooking technique unknown to Native Americans
___8. crawfish	h. used in moles for flavoring and thickening
___9. cuisine of the Southwestern United States	i. a global culinary style
___10. planked salmon	j. indigenous to the Gulf States

D. True or False: Circle either True or False to indicate the correct answer.

1. American cuisine, in both North and South America, is mostly a native culinary style.

    True   False

2. When Christopher Columbus and other explorers arrived in the Western Hemisphere, they found no established or advanced societies.

    True   False

3. The basic foods in the Americas include corn, bean, and squashes.

    True   False

4. Only two types of beans were grown and eaten throughout the Americas.

    True   False

5. The Europeans brought with them a cooking style that relied upon hot oil: frying, a technique unknown to the native Americans.

    True   False

6. One of the best ways to understand American cuisine is to take a look at each of the major regions.

    True   False

7. American chefs are considered to be among the finest in the world.

    True   False

8. The English first colonized the area known as the Mid-Atlantic States.

    True   False

9. Some of the traditional dishes enjoyed throughout the mid-Atlantic include scrapple (cornmeal and pork mush), crab boil, and crab cakes from the Chesapeake Bay area.

    True   False

10. The Southwest states are a mixture of cuisines developed by early English and French explorers.

    True   False

UNIT 37 ANSWER KEY

A. Terminology

All definitions can be found in the text.

B. Fill in the Blank

1. Incan, Aztec, Mayan
2. Spanish, Portuguese, English, French
3. Mayan
4. corn
5. open fires, warm embers, hot stones
6. metal
7. wok, stir-frys
8. land bridge
9. of the sea, of the mountains
10. Brazil

C. Matching

1. i
2. g
3. e
4. b
5. c
6. a
7. h
8. j
9. f
10. d

D. True or False

1. False
2. False
3. True
4. False
5. True
6. True
7. True
8. False
9. True
10. False